MY DAY! MY DREAM! MY DESTINY!

Date:

To:

From:

Message:

You Can Do More Than Survive, You Can Succeed!

Your Study Room Is Under NEW! Management

"Food Is for the Body
Education Is for the Mind,
And Poetry Is for the Soul."

Sharon Esther Lampert

#1 Poetry Website for Student Projects
www.WorldFamousPoems.com
The Greatest Poems Ever Written
on Extraordinary World Events

The Restless Sunrise

A Streaming Golden Light
Enters In and Under the Windowsill

A Restless Sleeper
Is Awakened to New Beginnings

To Catch a Sunrise
The Dreamer Arises as the Light Bursts Forth

The Sunrise Lights Up the Sky
In Anticipation of a World

That Has Yet To Be Created.

Sharon Esther Lampert

Also By The Author

Student Empowerment Tools
for Academic Success

- EVERY DAY AN EASY A
- TOTAL RECALL: ACE EVERY TEST EVERY TIME
- Your Study Room Is Under New Management
- Smartgrades School Notebooks with 1000 Learning Tools
- WRITERS RUN THE WORLD: College English Bootcamp!
- LEARN ENGLISH

Parent Empowerment Tools
for Academic Success

- How to Parent for Academic Success
- Broken Wings Blocked Blessings

Teacher Empowerment Tools
for Academic Success

- The Silent Crisis Destroying America's Brightest Minds ("Book of the Month" Alma Public Library, Wisconsin)
- The Universal Gold Standard of Education
- How Does Learning Take Place

Psychological Empowerment Tools
for Academic Success

- Integration Therapy: 14 Steps to True and Everlasting Happiness
- How to Stop Paying for the Sins of Your Parents
- Lost, Bad, and Evil: The Root of All Evil Is Child Abuse

Children's Book
The Smartest Children's Book in the Whole World
Learn New Vocabulary with Color-Coded Words
SCHMALTZY: IN AMERICA EVEN A CAT CAN HAVE A DREAM
The Cat Who Helps Children Learn, Love, and Laugh
THE WORLD FAMOUS PIANO VIRTUOSO
BOOKWORM CHILDREN'S BOOK AWARD
schmaltzy.com

Your Study Room Is Under NEW! Management

SMARTGRADES
BRAIN POWER REVOLUTION
www.smartgrades.com

SMARTGRADES Success Strategy Study Skills, K-12

Your Study Room Is Under **NEW!** Management

©2023 @2009 by Sharon Rose Sugar. All Rights Reserved. No part of this book may be used or reproduced in any manner whatsoever without written permission, except in the case of brief quotations embodied in critical articles and reviews.

Hardcover ISBN: 978-1-885872-79-1
Paperback ISBN: 978-1-885872-80-7
E-Book ISBN: 978-1-885872-81-4

Library of Congress Catalog Card Number: 2009943358
UPC: 672180

SMARTGRADES books may be purchased for education, business, or sales promotional use.

To order books:
Ingram Global Distribution, Phone: 615-793-5000
Baker and Taylor, Phone: 800-775-1800

SMARTGRADES
BRAIN POWER REVOLUTION

www.Smartgrades.com
www.EverydayAnEasyA.com
www.PhotonSuperhero.com
www.BooksnotBombs.com
www.Schmaltzy.com
www.SharonEstherLampert.com
www.WorldFamousPoems.com

Book Interior and Cover Design By Sharon Esther Lampert
Illustrations: By Mark A. Hicks, illustrator. Used with permission.
For more information, please visit websites:
www.MARKIX.net and www.markix.net/4teachers.html

First Edition

Manufactured in the United States of America

Eight Goalposts of Education

1. Education: Knowledge!
2. Enlightenment: AHA!
3. Empowerment: Yes I Can!
4. Excellence: Mastery!
5. Emancipation: All Can Do!
6. Egalitarianism: Equal Rights!
7. Equality: New World Order!
8. Economic Stability: World Peace!

Sharon Rose Sugar
The Paladin of Education for the 21st Century

To earn your diploma, every teacher will ask you to perform the same four academic tasks over and over again,
day in and day out,
week in and week out,
and year in and year out.

1. Read a Chapter
2. Write a Paper
3. Solve a Problem
4. Take a Test

Sharon Rose Sugar
The Paladin of Education for the 21st Century

THIS BOOK SAVES LIVES

"The Silent Crisis Destroying America's Brightest Minds"
"Book of the Month" Alma Public Library, Wisconsin

READ, WRITE, SOLVE, TEST

Your Study Room Is Under New Management

SMARTGRADES
SUCCESS STRATEGY STUDY SKILLS

Our books include the **SMARTGRADES Learning Skills and Life Skills** that will empower you for personal success at home, academic success in school, and professional success in the workplace.

SMARTGRADES Time Management Skills:
- Homework Action Planner
- To Do List Tool
- Setting Priorities Tool
- Divide and Conquer Tool
- Estimate and Actual Time Log Tool
- Detours, Delays, and Distractions Tool

SMARTGRADES In-Class Skills:
- Prereading Tool
- Active Listening Tool
- Note Taking Tool
- Abbreviation Tool
- Questioning Tool
- Test Preview Question Tool

SMARTGRADES At-Home Skills:
- Organization Tool
- Smartgrades School Notebooks
- Study Room Tool
- Study Strategy Tool
- Subject Strategy Tool
- Power Study Snack Tool
- Manage Anxiety, Stress, and Depression Tool

SMARTGRADES Reading Skills:
- Speed Reading Tool
- Reading Comprehension Tool

SMARTGRADES Test Preparation Skills:
- Processing Tools for Instant & Total Recall to Ace Tests

SMARTGRADES Writing Skills:
- Outlining Tool
- Annotating Tool
- Summarizing Tool
- Paraphrasing Tool
- English Essay Tool
- Research Paper Tool
- Citation Tool
- Proofreading to Perfection Tool

SMARTGRADES Thinking Skills:
- Critical Thinking Tools
- Creative Thinking Tools
- Scientific Thinking Tools
- Mathematical Thinking Tools

SMARTGRADES On-Test Skills:
- Multiple Choice Tool
- Essay Exam Tool
- True False Tool
- Matching Tool
- Fill In the Blank Tool
- Identity Exam Tool
- Verbal Analogy Tool
- Oral Exam Tool
- Open Book Tool
- Take Home Tool
- Standardized Exam Tool (High School Edition)

SMARTGRADES Career Skills: (College Edition)
- Career and Personality Tool
- Summer Internship & Life Experience Tool
- Networking Tool
- Entrepreneur Tool
- Job Tool
- Career Tool

© 2000. All Rights Reseved. SMARTGRADES, www.smartgrades.com

Sugar's 7 Facts of Academic Success

Fact 1. Your Brain Is a Powerful Biological Machine
Put your hands on your head and feel your brain. Your brain is the most powerful biological machine in the world. This book is your instruction manual. It will show you how to maximize your brain power. Facts are food for the brain. You will spend most of your day eating facts and building your brain muscles. First, you will receive facts from your teacher. Second, you will process the facts using the new learning technology, 10 Step **SMARTGRADES Success Strategies**. Third, you will return the facts to the teacher in a essay, research paper, or on a test.

Fact 2. Eat Right for the Energy to Learn
Before you can feed your brain the facts, you have to feed your body with the energy to learn. Every meal requires whole grain fiber, protein, fresh vegetables, and fruits containing vitamins and minerals. To maximize your energy to learn, you will need sufficient sleep, good eating habits, and regular exercise. Junk food won't cut it. Avoid eating processed food loaded with sugar, salt, and chemicals that are devoid of wholesome vitamins and minerals.

Fact 3. The First Week of School
It only takes the first week of school for students to fall behind and start playing catch up. You have to learn how to manage your time, and make every hour count.

Fact 4. School Is All About the Facts, Not About You
Your job is to **RETRIEVE** the facts from the class notes, handouts, and textbook, and then **RETURN** the facts to the teacher in an essay, research paper, and on a test.

Fact 5. The 80/20 Rule
If you can send back 80% of the facts for a B grade, then you can send back the remaining 20% of the facts for an A grade. If you process the facts for long-term retention using the new learning technology, 10 Step **SMARTGRADES Processing Tools**, then you will have Instant & Total Recall of all of the facts and ace the test.

Fact 6. What Are the Critical Hours of the School Day?
- Class Time: 1 Hour (fixed)
- Test Time: 1 Hour (fixed)
- Regular Study Period: 2-6 Hours (variable & critical)

Fact 7. Every Day of the Week Is Test Preparation Day
Priority 1: Did you sleep well, eat right, and exercise for the energy to learn? IT TAKES LOTS OF ENERGY TO LEARN!

Priority 2: Do you have a **SMARTGRADES Planner** to manage your academic and personal life?

Priority 3: Do you have **SMARTGRADES School Notebooks** that contain learning tools to ace every test every time?

Priority 4: Right after class, did you write **Test Review Notes** and process the facts using your 10 Step **SMARTGRADES Learning Tools** for Instant & Total Recall to ace the test?

10 Step SMARTGRADES Success Strategy Study Skills

Step 1. Estimation	Step 6. Association
Step 2. Divide and Conquer	Step 7. Test Review Notes
Step 3. Active Reading	Step 8. Conversion
Step 4. Extraction	Step 9. Visualization
Step 5. Condensation	Step 10. Self-Test

SUPERHIGHWAY OF ACADEMIC SUCCESS

School Is All About the Facts.

The Facts Are Always on the Move.

In Class
Facts Move from a Blackboard into a Notebook.

At Home
Facts Move into a Test Review Note,
Homework Assignment, Essay, and Research Paper.

On Test
Facts Move Through Your Brain for Instant
and Total Recall and onto a Test.

Education Is Measured By Three Criteria:

In-Depth Comprehension
Long Term Retention
Mastery of the Material

Sharon Rose Sugar
The Paladin of Education for the 21st Century

THIS BOOK SAVES LIVES
"The Silent Crisis Destroying America's Brightest Minds"
"Book of the Month" Alma Public Library, Wisconsin

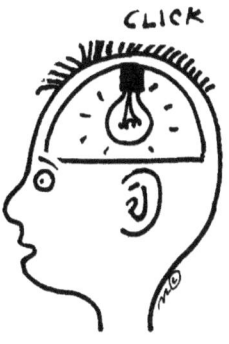

"Put Your Hands on Your Head.
Your Brain Is the Most Powerful
Biological Machine in the World.
Your Brain Is Your Most Valuable Asset.
This Book Is the Instruction Manual for Your Brain.

Facts Are Food for Your Brain.
School Is a Restaurant and Facts Are on the Menu.
Eat the Facts and Build Your Brain Muscle.
Knowledge Is Power, Purpose, Passion, and Prosperity.
Good Grades Deserve Great Rewards!
Earn A Grade, Earn Free Gift!

Make the Grade and Achieve Your Dream.
Every Student Is a Success Story.
Every Student Is Somebody Special.
Take Control of Your Destiny.
Live Your Dreams."

If You Need My Help, I Am at Your Service,

www.BooksnotBombs.com

MY DAY!
MY DREAM!
MY DESTINY!

Contents

Chapter 1
Your Study Room
23

Chapter 2
Your School Supplies
33

Chapter 3
Your Study Schedule
41

Chapter 4
Your Power Study Snacks
55

Chapter 5
Your Test Preparation Tools
**10 STEP SMARTGRADES LEARNING TOOLS
ACE EVERY TEST EVERY TIME**
63

Chapter 6
Your Writing Assignments
101

Chapter 7
Your Thinking Tools
143

Chapter 8
What Do You Want to Be When You Grow Up?
169

About Us
177

A Room Without Books Is Like a Body Without a Soul

Marcus Tullius Cicero

Chapter 1
Your Study Room

A Place for Everything, Everything in Its Place

Benjamin Franklin

Your Study Room

Tools of the Trade
Room with No External Distractions
Gather All Study Materials:
Class Notes, Handouts, and Textbook
Smartgrades School Notebooks
Power Study Snacks for the Energy to Learn
First Test Preparation, then Homework Assignments
Manage Your Time

Steps to Success

Right after school, you will go directly to your favorite study room and write your **Test Review Notes**. You will read your class notes, handout, and textbook and use your 10 Step **SMARTGRADES SUCCESS STRATEGY** to process (absorb) the facts for Instant & Total Recall to ace every test every time (Chapter 5).

Choose a Well Equipped Study Room

☐ 1. Choose a study room with no external distractions

☐ 2. Spacious desk for notebook, textbook, and reference materials

☐ 3. Sit in a comfortable chair that fits your body type

☐ 4. Good lighting

☐ 5. Computer with internet connection, printer, ink, and paper

☐ 6. External hard drive for daily backups of schoolwork

☐ 7. Pens, pencils, stapler, tape, paper clips, and ruler

Gather All of Your Study Materials

Example
Math Class
1. Class Notes, Handouts, and Textbook (3 sets of facts)
2. Smartgrades School Notebook with Success Strategies
3. Folder for Homework Assignments, Quizzes, and Tests

English Class
1. Class Notes, Handouts, and Textbook (3 sets of facts)
2. Smartgrades School Notebook with with Success Strategies
3. Folder for Homework Assignments, Quizzes, and Tests

Science Class
1. Class Notes, Handouts, and Textbook (3 sets of facts)
2. Smartgrades School Notebook with with Success Strategies
3. Folder for Homework Assignments, Quizzes, and Tests

History Class
1. Class Notes, Handouts, and Textbook (3 sets of facts)
2. Smartgrades School Notebook with with Success Strategies
3. Folder for Homework Assignments, Quizzes, and Tests

Language Class
1. Class Notes, Handouts, and Textbook (3 sets of facts)
2. Smartgrades School Notebook with with Success Strategies
3. Folder for Homework Assignments, Quizzes, and Tests

Computers Class
1. Class Notes, Handouts, and Textbook (3 sets of facts)
2. Smartgrades School Notebook with with Success Strategies
3. Folder for Homework Assignments, Quizzes, and Tests

Business Class for Entrepreneurship
1. Class Notes, Handouts, and Textbook (3 sets of facts)
2. Smartgrades School Notebook with with Success Strategies
3. Folder for Homework Assignments, Quizzes, and Tests

Right After School, Write Your Test-Review Notes

Facts are food for the brain. You cannot stuff a whole sandwich into your mouth. You have to take small bites and chew, chew, chew, and digest. The same holds true for the facts. You cannot stuff voluminous academic facts into your brain the night before the test and expect to ace the test. Right after school, you will write Test-Review Notes (Chapter 5) using the new learning technology, **SMARTGRADES Success Strategies** and process (absorb) the facts for Instant & Total Recall (long-term retention) to ace your tests. For each class, you will have three sets of Test-Review Notes, as follows:

Example: Write Test-Review Notes for All Classes
Math Class
1. Class Notes + Test-Review Notes (Chapter 5)
2. Handouts + Test-Review Notes
3. Textbook + Test-Review Notes

English Class
1. Class Notes + Test-Review Notes
2. Handouts + Test-Review Notes
3. Textbook + Test-Review Notes

Science Class
1. Class Notes + Test-Review Notes
2. Handouts + Test-Review Notes
3. Textbook + Test-Review Notes

History Class
1. Class Notes + Test-Review Notes
2. Handouts + Test-Review Notes
3. Textbook + Test-Review Notes

First Test Preparation, Then Homework Assignments

Test Preparation: 80% of Grade
Homework Assignments: 20% of Grade

Study Period: Test preparation is your first priority. Your second priority is to write Test-Review Notes. Your third priority is to complete your homework assignments. Your fourth priority is to proofread all of your written work. Your fifth priority is to preread the textbook chapter for your next class.

Set Your Study Priorities
- ☐ Priority 1. Test Preparation   80% of Grade
- ☐ Priority 2. Write Test-Review Notes   80% of Grade
- ☐ Priority 3. Homework Assignments   20% of Grade
- ☐ Priority 4. Proofread All Written Work
- ☐ Priority 5. Preread Textbook Chapter for Tomorrow

Example
Priority 1. Test Tomorrow
Priority 2. Write Test-Review Notes
Priority 3. English Essay Due Friday
Priority 4. Homework Assignments   20% of Grade
Priority 5. Proofread All Written Work
Priority 6. Preread Textbook Chapter for Tomorrow

Example
Priority 1. Test Tomorrow
Priority 2. English Essay Due Tomorrow
Priority 3. Write Test-Review Notes
Priority 4. Homework Assignments   20% of Grade
Priority 5. Proofread All Written Work
Priority 6. Preread Textbook Chapter for Tomorrow

Example
Priority 1. Test on Friday
Priority 2. English Essay Due Tomorrow
Priority 3. Write Test-Review Notes
Priority 4. Homework Assignments   20% of Grade
Priority 5. Proofread All Written Work
Priority 6. Preread Textbook Chapter for Tomorrow

Example
Priority 1. Test Next Week
Priority 2. Write Test-Review Notes
Priority 3. English Essay Due Friday
Priority 4. Homework Assignments   20% of Grade
Priority 5. Proofread All Written Work
Priority 6. Preread Textbook Chapter for Tomorrow

Example
Priority 1. Test in Two Weeks
Priority 2. Write Test-Review Notes
Priority 3. English Essay Due Friday
Priority 4. Homework Assignments   20% of Grade
Priority 5. Proofread All Written Work
Priority 6. Preread Textbook Chapter for Tomorrow

Example
Priority 1. English Essay Due Tomorrow
Priority 2. Test in a Month
Priority 3. Write Test-Review Notes
Priority 4. Homework Assignments   20% of Grade
Priority 5. Proofread All Written Work
Priority 6. Preread Textbook Chapter for Tomorrow

Tip: You can always ask your teacher for a time extension to complete a homework assignment, but not for a test.

How to Preread a Textbook Chapter

Before class, preread the textbook chapter to increase your understanding and absorption of the academic material.

Step 1. Read the End-of-Chapter Summary
Read the end-of-chapter summary for an overview of the main points of the chapter.

Step 2. Read the Boldface Headings of the Chapter
Read for a general overview of the material of the chapter. Read the boldface headings and subheadings. Read actively with a pencil/highlighter in hand and write down the main idea and major and minor points of the chapter.

Main Idea:

Major Points:
1.
2.
3.

Minor Points:
1.
2.
3.

After Class Read Textbook for In-Depth Comprehension
After school, you will go back to your class notes, handouts, and textbook and read for in-depth comprehension and write Test-Review Notes. You will use your, 10 Step **SMARTGRADES Success Strategies** to process the academic material for Instant & Total Recall to ace your exams (Chapter 5).

Your Teacher's Office Hours

Here are nine very good reasons to visit your teacher:

- ☑ Visit 1: Introduction
  Visit your teacher to introduce yourself.

- ☑ Visit 2: Seek Clarification
  Visit your teacher to ask a question.

- ☑ Visit 3: Approval of Topic and Outline of Paper
  Visit your teacher for approval of topic and outline of your paper.

- ☑ Visit 4: Approval of Rough Draft of Paper
  Visit your teacher for approval of rough draft of your paper.

- ☑ Visit 5: Teacher's Comments
  Visit your teacher to discuss comments on your paper.

- ☑ Visit 6: Unfair Test Question
  Visit your teacher to complain about an unfair test question.

- ☑ Visit 7: Grading Error
  Visit your teacher to complain about a grading error.

- ☑ Visit 8: Express Gratitude
  Visit your teacher to say thank you to express your appreciation for a great class.

- ☑ Visit 9: Recommendation for Your Resume
  Visit your teacher to ask for a recommendation to accompany your resume.

For Every Minute Spent Organizing, an Hour is Earned

Chapter 2
Your School Supplies

Don't Agonize, Organize!
Florynce R. Kennedy

Your School Supplies
Take Control of the Facts
Organize the Mountain of Academic Materials

Take control of the facts. School is a game of facts. Your job is to **RETRIEVE** the facts and **RETURN** the facts. First, you will retrieve the facts from the blackboard (class notes), handouts, and textbook, and then you will return the facts to the teacher in an essay, research paper, and on a test. You need to have an organization system in place to manage the voluminous academic facts.

For Example
Class: English
The academic facts come from 3 sources:
1. Class Notes
2. Handouts
3. Textbook

For each set of facts, you will write Test Review Notes. You will now have 3 sets of Test Review Notes:
1. Class notes + Test-Review Notes
2. Handouts + Test-Review Notes
3. Textbook + Test-Review Notes
4. Homework Assignments, Quizzes, and Tests

All of These Academic Materials Need to Be Organized

Your Study Room Is Under New Management

| Test Review Notes for Class notes | Test Review Notes for Textbook |

Blue Folder 1/English

| Class Handouts | Test Review Notes for Handouts |

Blue Folder 2/English

| Homework Assignments | Quizzes and Tests |

Blue Folder 3/English

Option 1. Cheap School Notebooks & Color-Coded Folders

Buy a school notebook for each class and buy color-coded folders to keep track of the following:
1. Test Review Notes (class notes, handouts, and textbook)
2. Quizzes
3. Tests
4. Homework Assignments

Buy Color-Coded Folders for Each Class:
English   Blue Folder
Math   Green Folder
Science   Yellow Folder
History   Purple Folder
Language   Red Folder

Label Your Blue Folders (3 Folders Per Class)
Folder 1. Test Review Notes
Pocket 1. Class Notes Test-Review Notes
Pocket 2. Textbook Test Review Notes

Folder 2. Class Handouts
Pocket 1. Handouts
Pocket 2. Test-Review Notes for Handouts

Folder 3. Homework, Quizzes, and Tests
Pocket 1. Homework Assignments
Pocket 2. Quizzes and Tests

SMARTGRADES
School Notebooks
Good Grades Become Grand Dreams
www.smartgrades.com

Class Notes and Test-Review Notes in One Notebook
How to Ace Every Test Every Time
How to Ace a Multiple Choice Test
How to Ace an Essay Test
How to Write a Research Paper
Homework Action Planners

BEFORE YOUR NEXT TEST, INVEST IN THE ACADEMIC BEST

SMARTGRADES BRAIN POWER REVOLUTION

Option 2. Buy the Best: Smartgrades School Notebooks

You can take class notes and write Test Review Notes in the same notebook, and the new learning technology, 10 Step **SMARTGRADES Processing Tools**, is at your fingertips. There is also a notebook for textbook Test Review Notes and research papers.

Manage Your Day, Your Dream and Your Destiny!
• The **SMARTGRADES** Homework Action Planner

Notebook 1. Class Notes and Test Review Notes
• The **SMARTGRADES** School Notebook for Class Notes and Test Review Notes

Notebook 2. Textbook Test Review Notes
• The **SMARTGRADES** School Notebook for Textbook Test Review Notes

Notebook 3. Research Papers
• The **SMARTGRADES** Research School Notebook

Handouts and Test-Review Notes
• One color-coded folder for handouts and Test Review Notes

Homework, Quizzes, and Tests
• One color-coded folder for homework, quizzes, and tests

The SMARTGRADES Advantage

• Buy a **SMARTGRADES** School Notebook and keep the receipt

• **SMARTGRADES** 1000 learning tools at your fingertips to ace every test every time

• Earn A Grade, Earn Free Gift!
(mail in receipt as proof of purchase)

• **PHOTON SUPERHERO OF EDUCATION** will call you to congratulate you on your academic success.

**Don't Count Every Hour in the Day,
Make Every Hour in the Day Count!**

Chapter 3
Your Study Schedule

It is Our Choices, Harry,
that Show What We Truly Are,
Far More than Our Abilities

Professor Dumbledore

Tools of the Trade

SMARTGRADES Homework Action Planner

Multiple Schedules:
1. Eat for the Energy to Learn Schedule
2. Class Schedule
3. Study Period Schedule
4. Test Schedule
5. Exercise Schedule
6. Extra-Curricular Schedule
7. Family Chores Schedule
8. Free Time

Steps to Success

Step 1. Write a "DAILY ACTION PLAN"
Purchase a Smartgrades Academic Planner (fully loaded) to manage your time, school assignments, and personal life.

Step 2. Organize Your Multiple Schedules
Your life will revolve around eight different types of schedules and you will need to write them down, analyze them, and reconfigure them, so that there is a seamless flow between them, instead of conflict, confusion, and chaos.

Step 3. Design a Daily Study Period Schedule
The critical hours of the school day are right after school. You have to read your books, write your papers, and prepare to take a test.

Your Study Room Is Under New Management

Plan Your Work and Work Your Plan

Don't Wish For It, Work For It

Success Comes in Cans, Not Cants

Well Done Is Better Than Well Said

The Only Something You Get for Nothing Is Failure

When You Lose, Don't Lose the Lesson

SMARTGRADES BRAIN POWER REVOLUTION _____ 45

Write a Daily Action Plan

Eat Right for the Energy to Learn:
Fiber Breakfast: Power Lunch: Lite Dinner:

Daily Budget: $
Expense 1. $ Expense 2. $ Expense 3. $
Total Daily Expenses: $

Classes:
Subject: Time: Room:
Subject: Time: Room:

Study Period 1: (45 minutes each with 15 minute breaks)
Time: Study Area:
Eat a Power Study Snack to stay energized, e.g., Bran Muffin
• Read and Process the class notes, handouts, and textbook
• Write Test Review Notes (**SMARTGRADES** Processing Tools)

Daily Exercise Routine: Stretch, Aerobics, Weights, Stretch

Study Period 2: (45 minutes each with 15 minute breaks)
• Seek approval from teacher for outline of paper
• Preread tomorrow's chapter for MAX absorption

Read a Daily Funny for Stress-Relief: "HA, HA, HA"

Part-Time Job:

Family Chores:

Social Life:

Regular Bedtime: 10 p.m.   Actual Bedtime:

Daily Reward for a Job Well Done:

Best Part of Day:

Worst Part of Day: Delays, Detours, and Distractions?

My Multiple Schedules Worksheet

Schedule 1. Eat Right for the Energy to Learn (variable)
M: Whole grains, protein, fresh fruits, and vegetables
T:
W:
TH
F:
S:
S:

Schedule 2. Class Schedule (fixed)

M:

T:

W:

TH:

F:

Schedule 3. Study Periods (variable)
M: Right after school, write your Test Review Notes
T:
W:
TH:
F:
S:
S:

Schedule 4. Test Schedule (fixed)
M:
T:
W:
TH:
F:
S:
S:

Schedule 5. Family Responsibilities (variable)
M:
T:
W:
TH:
F:
S:
S:

Schedule 6. Extra-Curricular Activities (fixed)
M:
T:
W:
TH:
F:
S:
S:

Schedule 7. Playdates (variable)
M: School night
T: School night
W: School night
TH: School night
F:
S:
S:

Schedule 8. Free Time (variable and negligible)
M:
T:
W:
TH:
F:
S:
S:

How to Design a Study Schedule

The ideal study schedule has 45-Minute study periods and 15-Minute study breaks to rest your eyes, stretch your legs, and eat a Power Study Snack (fiber fuel, e.g., bran muffin).

Example
4-4:45 p.m.
Math Homework
45 Minutes
15 Minute Break: Stretch, Eat a Power Study Snack

5-5:45 p.m.
Science Homework
45 Minutes
15 Minute Break: Stretch, Eat a Power Study Snack

6-6:45 p.m.
DINNER: 1/4 Protein, 3/4 Fresh Fruits and Vegetables

7-7:45 p.m.
English Homework
45 Minutes
15 Minute Break: Stretch, Eat a Power Study Snack

8-8:45 p.m.
History Homework
45 Minutes
15 Minute Break: Stretch, Eat a Power Study Snack

9-9:45 p.m.
Proofread All Written Work to Perfection
45 Minutes
15 Minute Break: Stretch, Eat a Power Study Snack

10-11 p.m. Bedtime

How to Manage Your Time

Time cannot be saved. To manage your time, you will need to use "Time Logs" and record the "Estimated Time" (fantasy time) and the "Actual Time" (life's bumpy road of setbacks). You will also have to record the "Error Time" as well as the inevitable "Speedbumps" of "Delays, Detours, and Distractions."

Example
4-4:45 p.m.
Math Homework
45 Minutes
15 Minute Break: Stretch, Eat a Power Study Snack

Time Log
Estimated Time: 45 Minutes

Actual Time: 1 1/2 hours

Error Time: 45 Minutes

Speedbumps: Any Delays, Detours, and Distractions?
Delays:
On the way home from school, I bumped into my friend Harry who updated me on school gossip.

Detours:
The buzzer rang and it was the UPS man with a package for my mother.

Distractions:
My sister's birthday was today and I had to stop my math homework to sing "Happy Birthday" to her and eat a slice of cake.

Take Control of Your Social Life Schedule

Keeping in touch with friends takes time. Pick a time to chat with your friends. Don't answer the phone and interrupt your study period every time a friend calls to talk with you, unless that friend is your study buddy. Pick a time after your school work is completed to make your social calls and stay connected to your loved ones.

Examples:

1. Suzy called about making a plan to see a movie

Action Plan: Call her back at 9:30 P.M.

Time Log

Estimated Time: 10 Minutes

Actual Time: 1 1/2 Hours

Error: 1 Hour and 20 Minutes

Delays, Detours, and Distractions: School Gossip

Action Plan: Friday, 8 P.M. for movie, meet at cafe

2. Peter called to study for test, study buddy

Action Plan: Call him back at 7:45 P.M.

Time Log

Estimated Time:

Actual Time:

Error:

Delays, Detours, and Distractions:

Action Plan: Meet in school library, Tuesday, 2 P.M.

My Social Life Schedule (Variable)

Making new friends and keeping in touch with old friends takes time. Your friends will change over time and place.

Q: How often do you introduce yourself to a new person?
a. Daily   b. Weekly   c. Monthly   d. Yearly

Here's how to introduce yourself to a new person:
1. Smile and make eye contact.
2. Say "Hello."
3. Ask a simple question? "What time do you have?"
4. Offer a compliment: "I love your blue sweater."
5. Introduce yourself: "My name is . . ."
6. What's your name?
7. Find common ground:
a. New study buddy
b. New playdate
c. New teammate for sports
d. New movie friend, loves comedy

Great relationships are based on connection, chemistry, compatibility, caring, communication, companionship, and common ground. When you meet someone, take notes:
Q1: What kind of connection do we have?
Q2: Do we have chemistry?
Q3: Are we compatible?
Q4: Is there genuine affection between us?
Q5: Do we have common interests?
Q6: Do we have honest communication?

How to Develop a Study Group

Study groups can keep you and your friends on track for academic success. These groups help everyone because they facilitate the learning process by thinking out loud, sharing ideas, and learning from each other.

There are many benefits to forming a study group:
1. Improve your understanding of the material
2. Share your talents
3. Provide an emotional support system to motivate you
4. Learning can be drudgery and sharing the tedious task lessens the pain.

Tools of the Trade

How many students?
Who should be in the study group?
Where should you hold the study sessions?
How long should a study session be?
When should the study group meet?
Who is the leader of the group?
What are the objectives and goals?

Steps to Success

Step 1. How Many Students?
The best size for a study group is four to six people. Small groups don't have man power to get things done. Large groups are harder to manage.

Step 2. Who Are the Members?
The best study groups are composed of individuals who share the same interest in doing well in class and on tests. Everyone has different strengths and weakness. By participating in a study group you are able to benefit from the talents of other group members.

Step 3. Where Do We Meet?
Study group sessions should be held in a location where you can talk and bring your power study snacks. The best place is an empty classroom, office space or dining room table.

Step 4. How Long Do We Study?
Study group sessions should be not longer than two to three hours. If the study session is too short, you can't accomplish anything. If it is too long, you loose interest and focus. Its best to schedule breaks every 45 minutes for a ten minute study snack.

Step 5. When Do We Meet?
Try to meet at the same time and place each week. Creating a set routine will help each member to plan ahead and come prepare to each session.

Step 6. Who Is the Leader of the Group?
Each group study session should have a leader. Its the leaders responsibility to make sure that the group is focused and stays on track.

Step 7. What Are the Objectives of the Study Group?
Doing well in school is all about retrieving the facts from your class notes, handouts and textbook reading assignments, and then returning the facts on a test.
The facts have to processed (absorbed) for Instant & Total Recall to ace your tests.

Energy Is Eternal Delight!
William Blake

Chapter 4
Your Power Study Snacks

Your Study Room Is Under New Management

Q: Are You Hungry for the Energy to Learn?
Whole Grain High Fiber Breakfast
Power Lunch: (Big Plate)
Lite Dinner: (Small Plate)
Power Study Snacks

Power Study Snacks for the Energy to Learn

Learning requires a great deal of energy. Every two hours, you will need some nutrition. When you are hungry, you will start searching for food. You will waste a lot of time walking up and down the aisles of a supermarket, and will be tempted as a result of persuasive advertisements to choose some processed food in a plastic wrapper that is loaded with sugar and salt and is devoid of vitamins and minerals. Or you will succumb to eating greasy junk food that will leave you undernourished and fat. On one hand, you may need that walk to stretch your legs and get some fresh air. On the other hand, there are too many temptations, and you will waste too much time and spend more money than your budget allows.

Make a Daily Power Study Snack Plan:
M: Yogurt, granola, and fruit
T: Bran muffin in a variety of flavors
W: Turkey sandwich with red peppers and cheese
TH: Carrots and celery sticks with humus
F: Trail Mix: Almonds, walnuts, cranberries, raisins
• Always carry a bottle of water with you to stay hydrated.
• Avoid soft drinks loaded with sugar that make you fat.

How to Eat Right for the Energy to Learn

You are a biological machine that needs fiber fuel to be able to think, read, research, write, memorize, and test. Before you leave for school, you need to have a system in place to manage your energy needs.

The Fiber Facts
Whole Grain Foods = Long-Term Energy and No Cravings

My 30-Second Breakfast
- Grab a bran muffin (try a different flavor each day)
- Grab two hard-boiled eggs (protein)
- Grab fruit: banana, apple, and orange (vitamins)
- Grab a container of orange juice (hydration)

My One-Minute Breakfast
- A slice of whole grain toast, cheese, tomato (fiber)
- Grab two hard-boiled eggs (protein)
- Grab fruit: banana, apple, and orange (vitamins)
- Grab a container of orange juice (hydration)

My Five-Minute Breakfast (Breakfast of Champions)
- A bowl of delicious and creamy oatmeal, add walnuts, sliced banana, cinnamon, and maple syrup. Drink a glass of orange juice.

My Power Lunch (Big Plate)
Fill big plate with 1/4 fist-sized protein and 3/4 vegetables
Monday: Fish with spinach, carrots, grilled red peppers
Tuesday: Meat with broccoli, carrots, corn
Wednesday: Fish with spinach, carrots, cauliflower
Thursday: Meat with green beans, carrots, corn
Friday: Fish with spinach, carrots, grilled red pepper

My Lite Dinner (Small Plate)
Fill small plate with 1/4 fist-sized protein and 3/4 vegetables
1. Eat off of a small plate to reduce your portion size
2. Eat dinner before 7 P.M.
3. Fill up on salad, vegetable soup, steamed vegetables
4. Avoid fried, fatty, and greasy food
5. Avoid heavy foods that put you to sleep after a meal
6. Avoid foods with sugar that keep you up late at night
7. No caffeinated drinks after 5 P.M. (poor sleep)

My Power Study Snacks for the Energy to Learn
1. Golden delicious apples with peanut butter or cheese
2. Fresh berries with yogurt and nuts, add honey
3. Carrot and celery sticks with humus
4. Bran muffins (cranberry, banana, carrot, apple)

Make Your Own Food Plan for the Energy to Learn

My 30-Second Breakfast

Whole Grain Fiber (long lasting fuel, no cravings):

_____

Protein: _____

Vegetables: _____

Fruits: _____

Hydration (sugar free): _____

My One-Minute Breakfast

Whole Grain Fiber (long lasting fuel, no cravings):

_____

Protein: _____

Vegetables: _____

Fruits: _____

Hydration (sugar free): _____

My Five-Minute Breakfast

Whole Grain Fiber (long lasting fuel, no cravings):

_____

Protein: _____

Vegetables: _____

Fruits: _____

Hydration (sugar free): _____

My Power Lunch (Big Plate)

Protein: Fish/Meat/Beans _____

Vegetables: _____

Fruits: _____

Hydration (sugar free): _____

Low Fat Dessert: _____

My Lite Dinner (Small Plate for Small Portions)

Protein: Fish/Meat/Bean _____

Vegetables: _____

Fruits: _____

Hydration (sugar free): _____

Low Fat Dessert: _____

No Caffeine After 5 P.M. (poor sleep, tired next day)

My Power Study Snacks for the Energy to Learn

Monday: _____

Tuesday: _____

Wednesday: _____

Thursday: _____

Friday: _____

Saturday: _____

Sunday: _____

Failing to Prepare Is Preparing to Fail

When You Take a Test,
You Are Really Being
Tested on Two Things:

1. How Much You Know
About the Subject

2. How Much You Know
About Taking a Test

Success Is When Preparation Meets Opportunity

Chapter 5
Your Test Preparation Tools

**10 STEP SMARTGRADES PROCESSING TOOLS
ACE EVERY TEST EVERY TIME**
Test Review Notes
Power of Association Cues
How to Ace Your Test
Test Types

In 24 Hours, F Students Become A Students
Every Student Earns an A Grade on the Next Test
Every Student Is a Success Story
Every Student Is Somebody Special
Make the Grade and Achieve the Dream

Sharon Rose Sugar
The Paladin of Education for the 21st Century

THIS BOOK SAVES LIVES
"The Silent Crisis Destroying America's Brightest Minds"
"Book of the Month" Alma Public Library, Wisconsin

SMARTGRADES PROCESSING TOOLS
ACE EVERY TEST EVERYTIME
Process Facts for Instant and Total Recall
Write Test Review Notes
Ace Test

Are You Test Ready?

SMARTGRADES PROCESSING TOOLS
ACE EVERY TEST EVERY TIME

Step 1.   Estimation Tool
Step 2.   Divide and Conquer Tool
Step 3.   Active Reading Tool
Step 4.   Extraction Tool
Step 5.   Condensation Tool
Step 6.   Association Tool
Step 7.   Test Review Note Tool
Step 8.   Conversion Tool
Step 9.   Visualization Tool
Step 10. Self Test Tool

- Don't Cram Facts for Short Term Retention

- Process Facts for Long Term Retention

- Process Facts for Instant and Total Recall

SMARTGRADES PROCESSING TOOLS
ACE EVERY TEST EVERY TIME
Process Facts for Instant & Total Recall

Are You Test Ready?

Education is food for the brain. Students spend the entire day eating facts and building their brain muscles. If I give you a sandwich to eat, you cannot stuff the entire sandwich into your mouth. You have to take small bites and chew, chew, chew, and digest. Eating facts is like eating a sandwich. You have to take small amounts of information and chew (in-depth comprehension), chew (long-term retention), and chew (mastery of academic material).

Right after every school, go directly to your study area and write your Test Review Notes to process (absorb) the facts for Instant & Total Recall to ace your exams.

DAILY ACTION PLAN
1. Get up early enough eat a high energy fiber breakfast
2. Preread the textbook chapter for maximum absorption
3. Go to class to receive teacher's wisdom and experience
4. Go to study room and write Test Review Notes for class notes, handouts, and textbook.
5. Use your 10 Step SMARTGRADES Processing Tools to process the facts for Instant & Total Recall to ace your tests.

SMARTGRADES PROCESSING TOOLS

To ace your exams, you have to develop three critical skills:

RETENTION, RECOGNITION, RECALL

1. **RETENTION** is your ability to absorb the facts.

2. **RECOGNITION** is reading the test question and knowing the answer.

3. **INSTANT RECALL** is popping out an answer in a jiffy.

4. **TOTAL RECALL** is long term retention of all of the facts.

To acquire these 3 skills, you need **REVIEW** and **REPETITION**.

Here are the 5 R's of Test Preparation
REVIEW, REPETITION, RETENTION, RECOGNITION, RECALL

The academic facts have to be processed (absorption) for Instant & Total Recall to ace your test. You have to eat facts, just like you eat food. The facts have to be digested. ACANDY PROCESSING TOOLS is a 10 step learning tool for Instant & Total Recall of the facts. Let's define each of the following terms:

Step 1. Estimation Tool
Step 2. Divide and Conquer Tool
Step 3. Active Reading Tool
Step 4. Extraction Tool
Step 5. Condensation Tool
Step 6. Association Tool
Step 7. Test Review Note Tool
Step 8. Conversion Tool
Step 9. Visualization Tool
Step 10. Self Test Tool

SMARTGRADES BRAIN POWER REVOLUTION

Step 1. Estimation Tool
Every paragraph contains one main idea and many supporting details. If you have ten paragraphs, then you have ten main ideas.

Step 2. Divide and Conquer Tool
You have to process one paragraph at a time for Instant & Total Recall. You cannot stuff a whole sandwich into your mouth. You have to take small bites, chew, chew, chew, and digest.

Step 3. Active Reading Tool
When you read, you need to be holding a pencil like a fisherman holds a net over the water to capture a fish. You are fishing for the facts. Every fact is a test question.

Step 4. Extraction Tool
You job is to extract the main idea and supporting details of every paragraph: Who, What, Where, When, and Why.

Step 5. Condensation Tool
Your job is to condense the facts and make them easier to digest, absorb, and process for Instant & Total Recall.

Step 6. Association Tool
Association links the unknown fact to a known fact in your mind. This is the glue that makes the facts stick to you.

Step 7. Test Review Note Tool
Your class notes, handouts, and textbook have to be processed for Instant & Total Recall to ace your tests.

Step 8. Conversion Tool
The facts have to be converted into test questions.

Step 9. Visualization Tool
Q: What type of test question is best suited for the facts?

Step 10. Self-Testing Tool
You have to answer your test questions to make sure that you have Instant & Total Recall and can ace your tests.

Your Study Room Is Under New Management

Right After School, Write Your Test Review Notes

SMARTGRADES PROCESSING TOOLS

1. Estimation Tool
How Many Main Ideas?
Every paragraph contains one main idea and many supporting details. If you have ten paragraphs, then you have ten main ideas.

Example: Estimate Main Ideas
1 main idea per paragraph
10 paragraphs = 10 main ideas

Paragraph 1
Main Idea:

Paragraph 2
Main Idea:

Paragraph 3
Main Idea:

---

2. Divide and Conquer Tool
You have to process one paragraph at a time for Instant & Total Recall. You cannot stuff a whole sandwich into your mouth. You have to take small bites, chew, chew, chew, and digest.

Paragraph 1
Main Idea:
Supporting Details:
Condense Facts:
Association Cue for Instant & Total Recall:
Possible Test Question:

3. Active Reading Tool

When you read, you need to be holding a pencil like a fisherman holds a net over the water to capture a fish. You are fishing for the facts. Every fact is a test question. Underline the main idea and supporting details.

Example: Underline Main Idea and Supporting Details
Thomas Jefferson was an intellectual, statesman, and third president of the United States. Although Jefferson served as governor of Virginia, ambassador to France, secretary of state, vice president, and president, he is remembered in history less for the offices he held than for what he stood for.

---

4. Extraction Tool

You job is to extract the main idea and supporting details of every paragraph: Who, What, Where, When, and Why.

Example: Extract Facts
Thomas Jefferson was an intellectual, statesman, and third president of the United States. Although Jefferson served as governor of Virginia, ambassador to France, secretary of state, vice president, and president, he is remembered in history less for the offices he held than for what he stood for.

One Main Idea   Many Supporting Details

Main Idea: Thomas Jefferson, 3rd President of U.S.A.

Many Supporting Details:
- Held many offices
- President
- Vice President
- Ambassador
- Secretary of State

5. Condensation Tool
Your job is to condense the facts and make them easier to digest, absorb, and process for Instant & Total Recall.

Many Supporting Details:
- Held many offices
- President
- Vice President
- Ambassador
- Secretary of State

Example: Condense Facts
Held Many Offices = P/VP/AM/SS

---

6. Association Tool for Instant & Total Recall
Association links the unknown fact to a known fact in your mind. Choose the Association Cue that works best for you. Personal memory is the most powerful Association Cue.

Example: Associate Facts
P/VP/AM/SS = Association Cue = Personal Memory

My Personal Association Cue Is:
PVP played on AM radio on weekends (Sat, Sun)
Totally ridiculous memory cue, but it works for me

---

7. Test Review Note Tool
Your class notes, handouts, and textbook have to be processed for Instant & Total Recall to ace your tests.
- ☐ a. Test Review Note for Class Notes
- ☐ b. Test Review Note for Handouts
- ☐ c. Test Review Note for Textbook Chapter

My Test Review Note
Main Idea:
Supporting Details:
Condense Facts:
Association Cue for Instant & Total Recall:
Possible Test Question

---

8 & 9. Visualization and Conversion Tool
Visualize test question and convert facts, the main idea, and supporting details into a sample test question.

Q: What type of test question is best suited for the facts?

Sample Test Question
Q: What positions did Thomas Jefferson hold?
(a) 3rd President of U.S.A.
(b) Governor of Virginia
(c) Ambassador to France
(d) Secretary of State U.S.A.
(e) Vice President of U.S.A.
(g) All of the Above

---

10. Self-Testing Tool for Instant & Total Recall
To ace a test, you need to process (absorb) the facts for long-term retention. Cramming facts for short-term retention does not work because you won't have Instant & Total Recall of the facts and you will not ACE your test.

Q: Can you recall the facts in a jiffy for Instant Recall?
Q: Can you recall all of the facts for Total Recall?

If you can't remember the fact, change the association cue.

Write Daily Test Review Notes:
Time Log
Estimate: 5 Hours
Actual:
Error:
Speedbumps: Delays, Detours, or Distractions?

How to Associate Facts for Instant & Total Recall

The facts have to be processed for Instant & Total Recall to ace your test. To process the facts for long-term retention, you have to link the **UNKNOWN** fact to a **KNOWN** fact in your mind. This linking process is called Association.
For example, here are two unknown words:

$$\text{Yin} \quad \text{Yan}\textbf{g}$$

One of these words is male and the other word is female. The word Yang is male. To process the fact for Instant & Total Recall, we want to associate the fact, that is link the **unknown** fact to a **known** fact in our mind.

	Association	
Unknown Fact	LINK	**Known** Fact in Mind
Yan**g** (male)	LINK	"g looks like a penis"

The letter "g' on the Yang looks like a male penis. You will remember this fact in an Instant and you will remember this for a lifetime. We linked the **unknown** fact to a **known** fact in your mind. This is how to achieve **Instant & Total Recall** of the facts.

Steps to Success

Step 1. Selection
Select facts to memorize: Main ideas and Supporting Details (who, what, where, when why, and how).

Step 2. Association
Choose the association cue that fits your learning style.

Acronym Cue: Use letters to condense the key facts. For example, to remember how to shoot a rifle, use the classic acronym BRASS, which stands for: Breath, Relax, Aim, Sight, Squeeze.

Acrostic Cue: Use a sentence to condense the key facts. For example, to remember the order of G-clef notes on sheet music, (E, G, B, D, F) use the classic acrostic: Every Good Boy Deserves Fun.

Rhyme Cue: Use rhymes to link the key facts together. For example, the classic, "I before E, except after C."

Music Cue: Make up a song or poem with the information in it. Sing the song or recite the poem several times.

Chaining Cue: Create a story where each word or idea you have to remember cues the next idea you need to recall. Use your imagination. If you had to remember the name, Shirley Temple, you could rhyme Shirley with curly and remember that she had curly hair around her temples.

Funny Cue: Write a joke that contains the key facts. The funniest, most outlandish, and the strangest concoction of memory cues makes memorizing easy.

SMARTGRADES PROCESSING TOOLS
My Test Review Notes to Ace the Test

Paragraph 1
• Extract Facts:
Main Idea:
Supporting Details:
a.
b.
c.

• Condense Facts:

• Associate Facts:

• Convert to Test Question:
Q: Who, What, Where, When, Why, How?

• Self-Test for Instant and Total Recall

Paragraph 2
• Extract Facts:
Main Idea:
Supporting Details:
a.
b.
c.

• Condense Facts:

• Associate Facts:

• Convert to Test Question:
Q: Who, What, Where, When, Why, How?

• Self-Test for Instant and Total Recall

Paragraph 3
• Extract Facts:
Main Idea:
Supporting Details:
a.
b.
c.

• Condense Facts:

• Associate Facts:

• Convert to Test Question:
Q: Who, What, Where, When, Why, How?

• Self-Test for Instant and Total Recall

Paragraph 4
• Extract Facts:
Main Idea:
Supporting Details:
a.
b.
c.

• Condense Facts:

• Associate Facts:

• Convert to Test Question:
Q: Who, What, Where, When, Why, How?

• Self-Test for Instant and Total Recall

"If any one faculty of our nature may be called more wonderful than the rest, I do think it is memory.
There seems something more speakingly incomprehensible in the powers, the failures, the inequalities of memory, than in any other of our intelligences. The memory is sometimes so retentive, so serviceable, so obedient; at others, so bewildered and so weak; and at others again, so tyrannic, so beyond control! We are, to be sure, a miracle every way; but our powers of recollecting and of forgetting do seem peculiarly past finding out."

Jane Austen

Read, Memorize, and Test

Tools of the Trade

Essay Exams
Multiple Choice Exams
True False Exams
Matching Exams
Fill in the Blank Exams
Oral Exams
Open Book Exams
Take Home Exams

Steps to Success

Step 1. The Day the Test is Announced

Q: Did you ask the teacher about the test?

a. What subjects are on the test?

b. What subjects are not on the test?

c. How many questions are on the test?

d. How is the test scored?

e. What kind of test is it?

Your Study Room Is Under New Management

Step 2. **Are You Prepared for the Right Type of Test?**
a. Essay Exam: Answer the question asked
b. Multiple Choice Exam: The answer is right in front of you
c. Oral Exam: Prepare for a personal interview format
d. Take Home Test: Apply ACANDY Critical Thinking Tools for in-depth analysis of the academic material (Chapter 10).

Step 3. **Two Weeks Before the Test**
Q: Did you review your Test Review Notes? (Chapter 7).
Q: Did you self test to find your strengths and weaknesses?
Q: Did you visit the tutoring center to work out problems?
Q: Did you transform your weaknesses into strengths?
Q: Can you recall the facts for Instant Recall?
Q: Do you remember all of the facts for Total Recall?
Q: Did you change the association cues that do not work?

Step 4. **The Night Before the Test**
Q: Did you review Test Review Notes for Instant & Total Recall?
Q: Did you get 8 hours of deep sleep to feel energized?
Q: Did you prepare pens, pencils, sharpener, calculator, tissues, and clothing?
Q: Did you set your alarm clock?

Step 5. **Manage Your Test Anxiety**
Anxiety and stress are debilitating. They will ZAP your energy and destroy your ability to focus and concentrate on the test and you will draw blanks.

Q: Did you practice deep breathing exercises to be able to maintain a calm composure and relax?

The 3-Breath Method of Relaxation Breathing
• Get in a comfortable position, spine straight, feet flat on the floor. Close your eyes.
• Concentrate on your body, and notice where there is tension, discomfort or stress.
• Take a deep breath, visualize all your stress, then breathe out. While breathing out, visualize all the stress leaving your body.
• Repeat these steps at least three times.

Step 6. Develop Your Self-Esteem with Positive Self-Talk
Q: When you listen to your inner voice, do you hear positive supportive messages, e.g., "I have the strength to make my dreams come true." On a daily basis, you need to develop your self-esteem with positive self-talk.
Examples
• Fear is only a feeling; it cannot hold me back

• I know that my potential is unlimited

• I have the strength to make my dreams come true

• I am proud of myself for even daring to try

• I grow in strength with every forward step I take

• I release my hesitation and make room for victory

Step 7. The Day of the Test
Q: Did you eat right (fiber fuel) for the energy to test?
a. Breakfast of Champions: Oatmeal with Fresh Fruit
b. Bran Muffin with Fresh Fruit

Q: Did you review your Test Review Notes to refresh your memory for Instant & Total Recall to ace your test?

The Day Before an Exam:
Prepare for the exam as if you are competing in an athletic event. Be well rested for the mental workout with a good night's sleep. Eat a high energy breakfast at least two hours before the exam, giving enough time for the body to digest the food. The day of the exam warm up the brain with a brief review. Arrive early. Relax. Compose your thoughts. Concentrate. Focus.

1. The Instructions:
First, listen carefully to oral instructions and then read all written instructions.

2. The Test Begins:
Jot down in the corner of the test everything you may forget during the test.

3. The Time:
Budget your time. Do not linger over difficult questions.

4. Your Mental, Emotional, and Spiritual Focus:
Concentrate on what you do know, don't worry about what you don't know.

5. The Question:
- Answer the questions you know first.
- Concentrate on one question at a time.
- Read each question completely before you begin to answer it.
- Answer question asked, not the one you may have expected.
- Go back to the ones you did not answer.
- Don't linger over difficult questions.
- Recall of the information you need may be triggered by completing other questions.

6. The Answer:
- Write down answer before reading choices.
- Read your answer choices carefully.
- Eliminate the choices that are clearly implausible.
- Don't search for hidden or extra meanings.
- Compare similarities & differences between choices.

Examine each word in answer for true or false possibility.
Key Words: All, Only, Always, Because = Generally False
Key Words: Few, Many, Much, Often, Many, Some, Perhaps, Generally = Possibly True
Break down complex sentences into smaller parts.
If small phrase = false, then entire statement = false.
If each word = false; then entire statement = false.

Change answers if you have a reason for doing so. However do not change your answers based on a whim. Use all the time allowed. If you finish early, proofread your paper for errors.

How to Ace Your Multiple Choice Test

Steps to Success

Step 1. Answer the easy questions first to build your confidence.

Step 2. Underline the key words in the question and try to answer the question. These tests rely on recognition, rather than recall.

Step 3. Think of multiple choice answers as a series of true or false statements. Read all of the choices even if the first choice seems correct. Compare similarities and differences between choices.

Step 4. Circle the absolute words in the question and the answer.

The absolutes are: all, none, always, never, only. These absolute words usually indicate a false choice.

Step 5. Circle the negative words in the question and the answer. Circle the negative words: not or except. These confusing questions cause careless errors. Mark each option with a T or F. Usually you are looking for a true statement. In this case, you are looking for a false statement.

Step 6. Find the dumb and dumber choices in the answer Cross out the two choices that are dumb and dumber. Examine the question and answer for clues.

Step 7. Change an answer when you have an intelligent reason to do so.

Beware the Dangers of Answer Sheets

Answer sheets allow exams to be scanned and marked automatically. Here are common mistakes to avoid:

1. Remember to record your name and student number on the actual answer sheet.

2. Use pencil so you can correct mistakes.

3. Do not cross out a mistake and mark another answer because the scanner will read this as "two" responses and record it as incorrect.

4. Always check your answers with the right question.

5. Consider marking your answers first on the exam paper, then transferring them to the answer sheet.

How to Ace Your Essay Test

Steps to Success

Step 1. Underline Key Word to Answer Question Asked

ANALYZE -- Find the main ideas and show how they are related and why they are important.

COMMENT ON -- Discuss, criticize, or explain its meaning as completely as possible.

COMPARE -- Show both the similarities and differences.

CONTRAST -- Show the differences.

CRITICIZE -- Give your judgment or reasoned opinion of something, showing its good and bad points. It is not necessary to attack it.

DEFINE -- Give the formal meaning by distinguishing it from related terms. This is often a matter of giving a memorized definition.

DESCRIBE -- Write a detailed account or verbal picture in a logical sequence or story form.

DIAGRAM -- Make a graph, chart, drawing. Be sure you label it and add a brief explanation if it is needed.

DISCUSS -- Describe giving the details and explaining the pros and cons of it.

ENUMERATE -- Name and list the main ideas one by one. Number them.

EVALUATE -- Give your opinion or some expert's opinion of the truth or importance of the concept. Tell the advantages and disadvantages.

ILLUSTRATE -- Explain or make it clear by concrete examples, comparison, or analogies.

INTERPRET -- Give the meaning using examples and personal comments to make it clear.

JUSTIFY -- Give a statement of why you think it is so. Give reasons for your statement or conclusion.

LIST -- Produce a numbered list of words, sentences, or comments. Same as enumerate.

OUTLINE -- Give a general summary. It should contain a series of main ideas supported by secondary ideas. Omit minor details. Show the organization of the ideas.

PROVE -- Show by argument or logic that it is true. The word prove has a very special meaning in mathematics and physics.

RELATE -- Show the connections between things, telling how one causes or is like another.

REVIEW -- Give a survey or summary in which you look at the important parts and criticize where needed.

STATE -- Describe the main points in precise terms. Be formal. Use brief, clear sentences. Omit details or examples.

SUMMARIZE -- Give a brief, condensed account of the main ideas. Omit details and examples.

TRACE -- Follow the progress or history of the subject.

Step 2. Restate Question as Introductory Sentence
Read the essay question and restate the question as the introductory sentence of your essay and add on the facts.

Example
Q: What are the most important issues your field is facing today?

A: The most important issues that my field is facing today are . . . add main ideas.

Step 3. Jot Down Main Ideas and Supporting Details
Jot down in the corner of the test the main ideas and supporting details to organize your thoughts before you write down the answer.

Main Ideas:
1.
2.
3.

Main Idea 1
Supporting Details:
1. Expert in Field
2. Indirect Quote
3. Examples
4. Analysis: Critical Thinking Tools
5. Sum It Up

Main Idea 2
Supporting Details:
1. Expert in Field
2. Indirect Quote
3. Examples
4. Analysis: Critical Thinking Tools
5. Sum It Up

Main Idea 3
Supporting Details:
1. Expert in Field
2. Indirect Quote
3. Examples
4. Analysis: Critical Thinking Tools
5. Sum It Up

Step 4. Use Standard Essay Structure
Use Introduction, Body, and Conclusion

Step 5. Use Standard Paragraph Structure
Sentence 1. Restate essay question ...
Sentence 2. According to Expert... (add quote)
Sentence 3. For example ... (proof)
Sentence 4. As a result ... (analysis)
Sentence 5. In conclusion ... (sum it up)

Step 6. Proofread Paper to Perfection
Proofread for spelling, punctuation, grammar, and neatness.

How to Ace Your True False Exam

Steps to Success

Step 1. Examine the Sentence

Every part of a true sentence must be "true." If any one part of the sentence is false, the whole sentence is false despite many other true statements. Long sentences often include groups of words set off by punctuation. Pay attention to the "truth" of each of these phrases. If one is false, it usually indicates a "false" answer.

Step 2. Underline Key Words

Pay close attention to negatives, qualifiers, absolutes, and long strings of statements.

Negatives: "No, Not, Cannot"
Qualifiers: "Sometimes, Often, Frequently, Ordinarily,
Absolutes: : "No, never, none, always, every, entirely, only"

Step 3: Guess True If You Are Unsure

Often true/false tests contain more true answers than false answers. You have more than 50% chance of being right with "true."

How to Ace Your Matching Exam

Steps to Success

Step 1. Use a Light Pencil

Mark them lightly with a pencil until you are completely done.

Step 2. Start with Matches that You Know Instantly

Step 3. Use a Darker Pencil

Make a second pass through matches, mark matches you are absolutely sure of with a darker penciled line.

Step 4. Search for Clues

Look for clues or relationships in the matches you aren't 100% sure of that you didn't think of the first time.

Step 5. Search for Other Possibilities

Look for another phrase that can be used instead of your first choice.

How to Ace Your Fill in the Blank Exam

Steps to Success

Step 1. This Type of Exam Is the Most Difficult and the Most Feared
You have to have the answers, such as names, places, and dates memorized for Instant & Total Recall.

Step 2. SMARTGRADES PROCESSING TOOLS
Use the new learning technology, SMARTGRADES PROCESSING TOOLS, to process (absorb) the facts for Instant & Total Recall and ace the test.

Step 3. Answer the Easy Questions First

Step 4. Underline the Key Words in the Question

Step 5. Other Questions May Jog Your Memory
Sometimes, answers to questions you don't know are supplied in other questions.

Step 6. Guessing
The chances of getting a correct answer by writing down a wild guess is very slim, although not entirely unlikely.

How to Ace Your True False Exam

Steps to Success

Step 1. Examine the Sentence

Every part of a true sentence must be "true." If any one part of the sentence is false, the whole sentence is false, despite many other true statements. Long sentences often include groups of words set off by punctuation. Pay attention to the "truth" of each of these phrases. If one is false, it usually indicates a "false" answer.

Step 2. Underline Key Words

Pay close attention to negatives, qualifiers, absolutes, and long strings of statements.

Negatives: "No, Not, Cannot"
Qualifiers: "Sometimes, Often, Frequently, Ordinarily,
Absolutes: "No, never, none, always, every, entirely, only"

Step 3: Guess True If You Are Unsure

Often true/false tests contain more true answers than false answers. You have more than 50% chance of being right with "true."

How to Ace Your Open Book Exam

Steps to Success

Step 1. Use Textbook and Test Review Notes
Since you have already condensed the facts from your textbook into Test Review Notes, they are probably the fastest way to access the facts.

Step 2. Use Standard Essay Format
a. Write in complete sentences.
b. Restate the essay question as the introductory sentence and add on the facts.
c. Use an Introduction, Body, and Conclusion
d. Use transition words to bridge ideas:

Sentence 1. On one hand ... (the Pro argument)
             On the other hand ... (the Con argument)
Sentence 2. According to expert... (add quote)
Sentence 3. For example ...
Sentence 4. As a result ... (analysis)
Sentence 5. In conclusion ... (sum it up)

Step 3. Proofread to Perfection
Check for spelling, grammar, punctuation, and neatness.

How to Ace Your Take Home Exam

Steps to Success

Step 1. What Kinds of Material Can Be Used?
Take Home exams are unrestricted. The main restriction for Take Home exams is that they must be your work–you must attempt them by yourself without any help from others.

Step 2. What Do Take Home Exams Test?
They don't test your memory. They test your ability to find and use information for problem solving, and to deliver well-structured and well-presented arguments and solutions. They require you to apply knowledge rather than just remember facts.

Step 3. Follow the Instructions for Open Book Exams

Step 4. Use SMARTGRADES CRITICAL THINKING TOOLS
To give a comprehensive analysis of the academic material, apply all of the SMARTGRADES Critical Thinking Tools (Chapter 7).

How to Ace Your Oral Exam

Steps to Success

Step 1. Create a Good Impression
- Dress well and appropriately
- Turn off your cell phone
- Arrive at the location early
- Review Test Review Notes
- Positive Self-Talk: "I am smartest banana in the bunch."

Step 2: Oral Exams Are Similar to Interviews
- Introduce yourself immediately and smile
- Give the instructor all of your attention
- Keep good posture and eye contact
- Stay focused through the exam
- Maintain your self-confidence and composure
- Be an intelligent listener as well as a talker
- Do not ramble if you do not know an answer
- If you do not know the answer, ask the teacher to ask the question in a different format to jog your memory
- Answer questions with more than "yes" or "no"
- Use two or three key points or examples to demonstrate your knowledge
- Thank the instructor

How to Transform an Exam Failure into a Success

You rushed through an exam, afraid that you will run out of time, and made careless mistakes:

- You misread the questions

- You misread the directions

- You blackened the wrong box on an answer sheet

- You skipped a question or two

- You forgot to write legibly

Steps to Success

Step 1. Ask for a Redo
An instructor may allow you to rewrite an essay exam, rework a math problem from the original question, and improve your grade. The worst they are going to say is no.

Step 2. Ask for Extra Credit Work
Ask for extra credit work to make up for a poor performance on a key exam.

Step 3. Review Mistakes
All knowledge bases are cumulative. Sometimes you get a problem wrong because you didn't understand the subject as well as you thought. After an exam fill in your knowledge gaps, to be prepared for the next test.

Step 4. Talk to Your Teacher
Ask your instructor for an explanation of your grade or comment. Use this as a time to find out how you can do better next time. Keep track of your strengths and weaknesses.

PHOTON'S
Introduction to Writing

Writing Is an Art Form
Creative Thinking Tools
Inspiration
Impregnation
Incubation
Genesis
Maturation
Revelation
Immortality

How to Write a Grade A Paper

Research Topic
Choose a Researchable Topic
Find Experts in Field
Use Direct and Indirect Quotes
Read Primary Source Material
List Pro and Con Arguments
Paraphrase Facts (in your own words)
Apply Critical Thinking Tools
Outline Main Ideas and Supporting Details
Writing is Rewriting: Rough Draft to Final Draft

Use Standard Paper Organization:
Introduction, Body, and Conclusion

Use Standard Paragraph Organization:
5 Sentences: Intro, Quote, Example, Analysis, Conclusion

Use Transition Words to Bridge Ideas:
According to, For example, As a result, In conclusion,

Add Citations: Footnotes or Endnotes
Add Bibliography

Proofread Paper to Perfection
Grammar, Spelling, Punctuation, Neatness

There's No Such Thing
As Good Writing.
There's Only Good Rewriting!

Mark Twain

I Hate Writing!
I Love Having Written!

Dorothy Parker

Chapter 6
Your Writing Assignments

English Essays
Research Reports
Proofreading to Perfection

English is a unique language. Why is the word phonetic not spelled the way it sounds? There's no egg in eggplant, no ham in hamburger, neither apple nor pine in pineapple. English muffins weren't invented in England nor French fries in France. Quicksand can work slowly, boxing rings are square, and a guinea pig is neither from Guinea, nor is it a pig. The plural of tooth is teeth, so why isn't the plural of booth beeth? If you wrote a letter, perhaps you bote your tongue? People recite at a play, and play at a recital; ship by truck, and send cargo by ship; have noses that run, and feet that smell; park on driveways, and drive on parkways. A slim chance and a fat chance mean the same, but a wise man and a wise guy are opposites. Overlook and oversee are opposites, while quite a lot and quite a few are alike. A house can burn up as it burns down, a form can be filled in by being filled out, an alarm clock goes off by going on. On the other hand, so to speak, some things are talked about only when they are absent; i.e., we do not hear about a horseful carriage or a strapful gown, a sung hero or required love, someone who is combobulated, gruntled, ruly, or peccable.

Unknown Internet quote

Write an A Grade Paper

Tools of the Trade

Research Topic
Choose Researchable Topic
Use Library Databases
Use Encyclopedia for General Overview
Find Experts in Field
Read Primary Sources (autobiographical)
Read Secondary Sources (biographical)
List Pro and Con Arguments
Paraphrase Research (in your own words)
Use Direct and Indirect Quotes
Document Source Material: MLA, APA, Chicago Style

Write Paper
Write Outline
Write Thesis Statement
Use Standard Paper Structure
Use Standard Paragraph Structure
Use Transition Words to Bridge Paragraphs and Ideas
Apply Critical Thinking Tools (Chapter 7, p.143)
Seek Teacher's Approval for Outline and Rough Drat
Write Final Draft
Add Citations: Footnotes or Endnotes
Add Bibliography
Proofread Paper to Perfection (p. 133)

Your Study Room Is Under New Management

There Are Four Basic Types of Essays:
Description, Narration, Exposition, Persuasion

Each of these types of essays has its distinctive characteristics; however, you will find that essays are often a combination of the various forms.

1. Expository
2. Descriptive
3. Explanatory
4. Illustrative
5. Analytical
6. Argumentative
7. Defining
8. Evaluative
9. Interpretive

Definitions of Essays

1. **Expository:** An essay to convey "information."

2. **Descriptive:** An essay that describes something or someone, a situation or a location.

3. **Explanatory:** An essay that looks for reasons or causes in relation to perceived effects or results based on theory.

4. **Illustrative:** An essay that is fairly descriptive, but illustrations need to be relevant and appropriate, and written with explicit reference to the theoretical point being supported.

5. **Analytical:** An essay for experimental data. It is the process of breaking down something into its component parts, often in order to analyse patterns or categories based on a theoretical position.

6. **Argumentative:** An essay of debate and disagreement.

7. **Defining:** An essay based on a definition of terms.

8. **Evaluative:** An essay that requires you to pass judgement or make an assessment, according to stated criteria.

9. **Interpretive:** An essay where your interpretation is examined in the context of other more established interpretations.

A Simple Overview of Essay Paper

Steps to Success

Step 1: Restatement of Essay Question

Read essay question and restate question as the topic sentence of essay.

Here is a sample essay question:

Q: If your doctor told you that you had only a few months to live, how would you alter your way of life? Discuss.

To answer this essay question, first restate the question as the introductory sentence of your essay, as follows: If (my) doctor told (me) that (I) had only a few months to live, (I) would alter (my) way of life by... add on the facts.

Step 2. Write Outline of Essay to Organize Thoughts

Write outline of main ideas and supporting examples.

Essay Outline

Main Idea 1. Spend more time with loved ones
Supporting Example: Take pictures for a lasting legacy

Main Idea 2. Visit the beautiful places on earth
Supporting Example: Take a trip to Hawaii

Step 3. Use Standard Essay and Paragraph Structure
Use standard essay structure: Introduction, body, and conclusion. Use standard paragraph structure: Experts, quotes, examples, analysis, and transition words.

Introduction	Introduce Topic
	Introduce Main Ideas 1, 2, and 3
Body	Paragraph 1
	Introduce Main Idea 1
	Add: Supporting Example
	Add: Direct or Indirect Quote
	Add: Analysis, Critical Thinking Tools
	Add: Concluding Sentence
	Add: Transition Words to Link Ideas
Body	Paragraph 2
	Introduce Main Idea 2
	Add: Supporting Example
	Add: Direct or Indirect Quote
	Add: Analysis, Critical Thinking Tools
	Add: Concluding Sentence
	Add: Transition Words to Link Ideas
Body	Paragraph 3
	Introduce Main Idea 3
	Add: Supporting Example
	Add: Direct or Indirect Quote
	Add: Analysis, Critical Thinking Tools
	Add: Concluding Sentence
	Add: Transition Words to Link Ideas
Conclusion	Restate Introduction and Main Ideas
	Final Thoughts

Research Topic

Tools of the Trade

How to Use Library Databases
Use Encyclopedia for General Overview of Topic
List Experts in Field
List Pro and Con Arguments
Read Primary Sources (Autobiographical)
Read Secondary Sources (Biographical)
Document Sources: MLA, APA, Chicago Style
Paraphrase Don't Plagiarize
Organize: Smartgrades Research School Notebook
Take Control of Your Time with Time Logs

Steps to Success

Step 1. Use Encyclopedia for General Overview of Topic
Q: Who are the experts in the field?
1. 1st Expert:

2. 2nd Expert:

3. 3rd Expert:

Step 2. Read Bibliographic Notes for a List of Primary and Secondary Source Materials on the Topic

Q: How many source materials are required for paper?

1. Primary Source (autobiographical):
Book:
Author:
Publisher:
Copyright:
Page #

2. Primary Source (autobiographical):
Book:
Author:
Publisher:
Copyright:
Page #

3. Secondary Source (biographical):
Book:
Author:
Publisher:
Copyright:
Page #

Step 3. Read Primary and Secondary Source Materials for Pro and Con Arguments and Quotes (Direct and Indirect).

1st Expert in Field:
Pro Argument:
Direct or Indirect Quote:
Citation: Book, Author, Publisher, Copyright, Page #

2nd Expert in Field:
Pro Argument:
Direct or Indirect Quote:
Citation: Book, Author, Publisher, Copyright, Page #

3rd Expert in Field:
Con Argument:
Direct or Indirect Quote:
Citation: Book, Author, Publisher, Copyright, Page #

Research Topic
Time Log
Estimate Time: 10 Hours
Actual Time:
Error:
Speedbumps: Any Delays, Detours, and Distractions?

Your Study Room Is Under New Management

Use Library Databases

Libraries are divided into reading rooms, restricted collections, and unrestricted book stacks.

Unrestricted Book Stacks:
- Anyone can use and read in the library, or take home

Restricted Collections:
- Special collections of rare books
- Open to Scholars, or to those with credentials

Libraries contain circulating and non-circulating materials for use only in the library, e.g., reference materials.

Step 1. Use Encyclopedia for General Overview of Topic
The leading encyclopedias are:
- Britannica
- Americana
- Collier's
- World Book

Step 2. Use Card Catalog for Primary and Secondary Sources
This is a list of all of the books in the library. The books are indexed by subject, author, and title.

Step 3. Use Newspaper Indexes for Most Recent News
Many large city newspapers provide an indexed list of all published articles.

Step 4. Use Periodical Indexes for Most Recent News
The most popular magazine articles are published in "The Readers' Guide to Periodical Literature."

Step 5. Use the Vertical File
This file contains pamphlets and brochures.

Step 6. Use the U.S. Documents Monthly Catalog
This is useful for locating government publications.

How is Your Library Organized

Most libraries use the Dewey Decimal Classification System. This system uses numbers 000-999 to classify all materials by subject matter.

The Dewey Classification System

000 - 099	General
100 - 199	Philosophy
200 - 299	Religion
300 - 399	Social Sciences
400 - 499	Language
500 - 599	Science
600 - 699	Useful Arts
700 - 799	Fine Arts
800 - 899	Literature
900 - 999	History

Library of Congress Classification System
This system uses letters to denote major categories.

A GENERAL WORKS
B   PHILOSOPHY. PSYCHOLOGY. RELIGION
C   AUXILIARY SCIENCES OF HISTORY
D   WORLD HISTORY AND HISTORY OF EUROPE, ASIA, AFRICA, AUSTRALIA, NEW ZEALAND, ETC.
E   HISTORY OF THE AMERICAS
F   HISTORY OF THE AMERICAS
G   GEOGRAPHY. ANTHROPOLOGY. RECREATION
H   SOCIAL SCIENCES
J   POLITICAL SCIENCE
L   EDUCATION
M   MUSIC AND BOOKS ON MUSIC
N   FINE ARTS
P   LANGUAGE AND LITERATURE
Q   SCIENCE
R   MEDICINE
S   AGRICULTURE
T   TECHNOLOGY
U   MILITARY SCIENCE
V   NAVAL SCIENCE
Z   BIBLIOGRAPHY. LIBRARY SCIENCE. INFORMATION RESOURCES (GENERAL)

Library Research
Time Log
Estimate: 20 Hours (Find Books, Read Books, Take Notes)
Actual Time:
Error:

Speedbumps: Any Delays, Detours, and Distractions?

Write a Thesis Statement

Tools of the Trade
Arguable Topic, Question, Point of View, Defense

What is a Thesis?

A thesis statement declares what you believe and what you intend to prove. An effective thesis has a definable, arguable claim. You must do a lot of background reading before you know enough about a subject to identify key or essential questions. You may not know how you stand on an issue until you have examined the evidence.

Steps to Success

Step 1. Select a Topic.

Example
Topic: Television sex and violence

Step 2. Ask an Interesting Question

Example
Q: What are the effects of television sex and violence on children?

Step 3. Write a Thesis Statement (Point of View)

Example: Thesis Statement
Sex and violence on television increases aggressive behavior in preschool children.

Step 4. Defend Your Thesis Statement
Choose arguments and evidence to defend your Thesis

Paraphrase Ideas of Others
How to Write it in Your Own Words

A paraphrase is restating the ideas of others in your own words and keeping the meaning intact.

Tools of the Trade

Original Source Material
"Unique Terminology"
Main Idea and Supporting Details
Keep Meaning Intact
Add Citation: Book, Author, Publisher, Copyright, Page #

Steps to Success

Step 1. Read original passage for in-depth comprehension.

Step 2. Write down main idea and supporting ideas.

Step 3. If you used any "unique terminology" from the passage put a quote around it.

Step 4. Cite the source to credit it.

Step 5. Rewrite original passage in your own words.

Example

Original Text

Aristotle is a Greek philosopher, scientist, and educator who lived from 384 to 322 B.C. He is considered one of the greatest and most influential philosophers in Western culture. He was born in northern Greece on the Macedonian coast, in a small town called Stagira.

List Main Idea and Supporting Details:
Main Idea: Aristotle, Greek Philosopher, Scientist, Educator
Supporting Details:
(a) 384 to 322 B.C.
(b) Born: Greece, Macedonian coast, town of Stagira
Citation: Encyclopedia

Paraphrase Text

One of the most admired and respected philosophers in Western culture was a man named Aristotle (384 to 322 B.C.). He was born in Greece in the small town of Stagira that is located on the Macedonian coast (citation: encyclopedia).

Paraphrase Source Material
Time Log
Estimate Time: 10 Hours
Actual Time:
Error:
Speedbumps: Any Delays, Detours, and Distractions?

Write Outline of Paper

Tools of the Trade

List Experts in Field
List Pro and Con Arguments
List Arguments from Most Important to Least Important
Add Citations: Book, Author, Publisher, Copyright, Page #
Organize: Smartgrades Research School Notebook
Take Control of Your Time with Time Logs
See Teacher for Approval of Outline

Steps to Success

Step 1. Write Outline of Paper
Estimate: Pages, Paragraphs, Main Ideas
- 3 Page Paper has 3 Paragraphs Per Page
- 3 Page Paper has a Total of 9 Paragraphs
- 9 Paragraphs: 1 Main Idea Per Paragraph
- 9 Paragraphs: 7 Main Ideas Plus Intro and Conclusion

The Outline

Page 1
Paragraph 1
Write Introductory Paragraph of Paper
Write a Thesis Statement (point of view to defend).

Paragraph 2
The Most Important Main Idea Is:
Supporting Experts, Quotes, Examples, and Analysis
Citation: Book, Author, Publisher, Copyright, Page #

Paragraph 3
The Second Most Important Main Idea Is:
Supporting Experts, Quotes, Examples, and Analysis
Citation: Book, Author, Publisher, Copyright, Page #

Page 2
Paragraph 4
Main Idea:
Supporting Experts, Quotes, Examples, and Analysis
Citation: Book, Author, Publisher, Copyright, Page #

Paragraph 5
Main Idea:
Supporting Experts, Quotes, Examples, and Analysis
Citation: Book, Author, Publisher, Copyright, Page #

Paragraph 6
Main Idea:
Supporting Experts, Quotes, Examples, and Analysis
Citation: Book, Author, Publisher, Copyright, Page #

Page 3
Paragraph 7
Main Idea:
Supporting Experts, Quotes, Examples, and Analysis
Citation: Book, Author, Publisher, Copyright, Page #

Paragraph 8
Main Idea:
Supporting Experts, Quotes, Examples, and Analysis
Citation: Book, Author, Publisher, Copyright, Page #

Paragraph 9
Write the Concluding Paragraph of Paper
Restate Main Idea and Supporting Ideas and Sum It Up

The Outline
Time Log
Estimate Time: 5 Hours
Actual Time:
Error:
Speedbumps: Any Delays, Detours, and Distractions?

Write Rough Draft of Paper

Tools of the Trade

Write a Thesis Statement
Choose Point of View and Defend Your Position

Use Standard Paper Organization:
Introduction, Body, and Conclusion

Use Standard Paragraph Organization:
Sentence 1. Introductory Sentence
Sentence 2. Expert in Field
Sentence 3. Direct or Indirect Quote
Sentence 4. Example, Evidence, Explanation
Sentence 5. Analysis (Critical Thinking Tools)
Sentence 6. Concluding Sentence

Use Transitions to Bridge Paragraphs and Ideas
According to, For example, As a result, In conclusion

Apply Critical Thinking Tools (Chapter 8, p.143)
Separate the Facts, Belief Systems, and Opinions
Distinguish Theory from Reality

Add Citations: Footnotes or Endnotes
Add Bibliography
Proofread to Perfection (p. 133)
Take Control of Your Time with Time Logs
See Teacher for Approval of Rough Draft

Steps to Success

Step 1. Use Standard Paper Format: Introduction, Body, and Conclusion

Step 2. Write the Introduction to Your Paper
Introduce topic, supporting ideas, and include thesis statement.

For Example: Title, Topic, Introduction, Thesis Statement

"The Mountain Lion:
Once Endangered, Now a Danger

On April 23, 1994, as Barbara Schoener was jogging in the Sierra foothills of California, she was pounced on from behind by a mountain lion (Rychnovsky 39). California politicians presented voters with Proposition 197, which contained provisions repealing much of a 1990 law enacted to protect the lions."

Write a Thesis Statement: Take Point of View and Defend
"A future proposition should retain the ban on sport hunting but allow the Department of Fish and Game to control the population. Wildlife management would reduce the number of lion attacks on humans and in the long run would also protect the lions."

Step 3. Write the Body of Your Paper
Follow your Outline and introduce one main idea per paragraph followed by supporting materials of experts in field, direct and indirect quotes, evidence, and sum it up.

Step 4. Write the Conclusion of Your Paper
Restate introduction and main ideas and sum it all up.

The Rough Draft of Paper
Time Log
Estimate Time: 25 Hours
Actual Time:
Error:
Speedbumps: Any Delays, Detours, and Distractions?
Visit Teacher for Approval of Rough Draft

Use Direct and Indirect Quotes

A quotation is a reference to an authority, or a citation of an authority. There are two types of quotations: direct and indirect.

Tools of the Trade

Experts in Field
Primary and Secondary Sources
Direct Quotes
Indirect Quotes, Paraphrasing, and Transition Words
Add Citations
Short Quotation Format
Long Quotation Format

You can choose to use either type of quote. Use quotes sparingly. Always provide a context for your quotations that explains to the reader why and how the quote is relevant to the topic.

Choice 1. Direct Quotation
A direct quotation uses the exact words of an authority, and must be documented with quotation marks and a citation.

Choice 2. Indirect Quotation
An indirect quotation, or paraphrase, is a restatement of a thought expressed by someone else that is written in your own words and must be documented with a citation.

Example: Direct Quote
Author John Smith argues that "More people are dying from medical errors than from fatal diseases" (citation).

Example: Indirect Quote (Paraphrase)
According to a recent report, medical errors are killing more people than disease (citation).

Example: Combine Indirect and Direct Quotations
According to a news recent report, medical errors can be fatal as substantiated by the author John Smith, who said, "More people are dying from medical errors than from fatal diseases" (citation).

Example: Use Transition Words for Introductions
You can introduce quotations with transition words, such as, " According to..." or "In sum," as illustrated by the following:

According to Professor John Smith, "add direct quote" (citation).

Professor John Smith **sums up** the situation in the following passage: "add direct quote" (citation).

Example: Short Quotation Format
If your quotations are less than four lines long, place them in your text, and enclose them with quotation marks. This quote begins with an introductory transition word, "According to..."

According to Confucius, "Respect yourself and others will respect you" (citation).

Example: Long Quotation Format
If your quotation is more than four lines long, set it off from your text by indenting. Introduce the quotation with a complete sentence and a colon. Indent ten spaces, double space the lines, and do not use quotation marks.

Confucius sums up the situation in the following passage:

The superior man, when resting in safety, does not forget that danger may come. When in a state of security he does not forget the possibility of ruin. When all is orderly, he does not forget that disorder may come. Thus his person is not endangered, and his States and all their clans are preserved (citation).

Use Direct and Indirect Quotes with Citations
Time Log
Estimate Time: 5 Hours
Actual Time:
Error:
Speedbumps: Any Delays, Detours, and Distractions?

Use Standard Paragraph Formation

Each Paragraph in a Paper is Composed of Five Parts:
Sentence 1   Introductory Sentence and Main Idea
Sentence 2-4   Direct/Indirect Quotes from Experts
Sentence 4-6   Supporting Arguments/Examples
Sentence 6-8   Analysis (Critical Thinking Skills)
Last Sentence   Summation or Concluding Sentence

Step 1. Write the Main Idea Sentence:
According to Professor X ... (direct/indirect quote)

Step 2. Write Supporting Sentences to Defend Your Position: For example, ...

Step 3. Use Transition Words to Link Ideas
In addition, ...   Furthermore, ...   Moreover,...

Step 4. Write the Analysis Sentences:
As a result, ...
Use SMARTGRADES Critical Thinking Tools (Chapter 7, p.143)

Step 5. Write Concluding Sentence:
In sum, ...

Use Transition Words

Transition Words Link Ideas Within Paragraphs
and Build Bridges Between Paragraphs

Transitions are words and phrases that guide a reader from one idea to the next. Use words sparingly.

To begin a sentence: However, nevertheless, furthermore, therefore

To give examples: As, for example, for instance, In other words, like, such as, that is

For causes: Accordingly, because, due to, for this, for that reason, if ...then, since

For effects: As a result, consequently, for, nevertheless, owing to, so that, therefore, so, thus

For comparisons (similarities): Along with, also, as, besides, both, furthermore, in comparison, in the same way, just as, likewise, moreover, similarly

To add an idea: Again, also, and, furthermore, equally, in addition, moreover

For contrasts (differences): Although, but, by contrast, different from, however, in contrast, instead, nevertheless, on the one hand, on the other hand, rather than, unlike, whereas, yet

For order of importance: All, best, better, first, last, least important, less important, most importantly, most of second, strongest, third, weakest

For temporal order (time): After, as soon as, before, during, finally, first, last, later, meanwhile, next, now, second, since, soon, suddenly, then, third, whenever, while, until, yesterday

For spatial order (place): Above, across, along the side, around, behind, below, beside, center, here, inside, on top of, to the left, in front of, outside, opposite, near, next to, to the center, to the right, there, where

For endings: As a result, finally, in conclusion, in summation

Use Proper Citation Style to Document Sources

Tools of the Trade

MLA Style: Writing in English and Humanities
APA Style: Writing in the Social Sciences
Chicago Style: Writing in History and Humanities

There are two reasons to document your source material:

Reason 1. Show readers where you obtained your facts.

Reason 2. Give readers a list of references should they want to read more about the subject.

Steps to Success

- Cite a source to give the origin of facts or opinions

- Cite a source when using a direct quote

- Cite a source when paraphrasing someone else's work

- Cite a source when stating an unknown fact

- Cite a source when stating controversial facts

Use Citation Format to Document Sources

Tools of the Trade
Footnotes/Endnotes
Parenthetical References

Footnotes and endnotes are basically the same thing — each provides information about where you found the material for your research paper. The only difference is where you put them in your research paper. If you use a quote from a book, you would put a footnote at the bottom (the foot) of the page that the quote appears on, citing the source of the quote. If you're using endnotes instead of footnotes, the endnote would go in a list at the end of the paper with all the other endnotes.

Example: Footnote or Endnote
1- M.I. Finley, "The Silent Women of Rome," in Horizon, no 7 (1965), Tuscaloosa, Horizon Publishers, p. 64.

Parenthetical references are brief citations, enclosed by parentheses, within the text of the paper.

Example: Parenthetical Reference
Shelley thought poets "the unacknowledged legislators of the world" (Magill 2001).

Use Endnotes, Footnotes or Parenthetical References
Time Log
Estimate Time: 5 Hours
Actual Time:
Error:
Speedbumps: Any Delays, Detours, and Distractions?

How to Write a Bibliography

Tools of the Trade

Author (last name first)
Title of Book
City: Publisher
Date of Publication

Steps to Success

1. For a Book
Author (last name first). Title of the book. City: Publisher, Date of publication.

Example:
Dahl, Roald. The BFG. New York: Farrar, Straus and Giroux, 1982.

2. For an Encyclopedia:
Encyclopedia Title, Edition Date. Volume Number, "Article Title," page numbers.

Example:
The Encyclopedia Britannica, 1997. Volume 7, "Gorillas," pp. 50-51.

3. For a Magazine:
Author (last name first), "Article Title." Name of magazine. Volume number, (Date): page numbers.

Example:
Jordan, Jennifer, "Filming at the Top of the World." Museum of Science Magazine. Volume 47, No. 1, (Winter 1998): p. 11.

4. For a Newspaper:
Author (last name first), "Article Title." Name of newspaper, city, state of publication. (date): edition if available, section, page number(s).

Example:
Powers, Ann, "New Tune for the Material Girl." The New York Times, New York, NY. (3/1/98): Atlantic Region, Section 2, p. 34.

5. For World Wide Web:
URL (Uniform Resource Locator or WWW address). author (or item's name, if mentioned), date.

Example: (Boston Globe's www address)
http://www.boston.com. Today's News, August 1, 1996.

6. For a CD-ROM:
Disc title: Version, Date. "Article title," pages if given. Publisher.

Example:
Compton's Multimedia Encyclopedia: Macintosh version, 1995. "Civil rights movement," p.3. Compton's Newsmedia.

Write Final Draft of Paper

Tools of the Trade

Proofread Paper to Perfection (p. 133)

- Check Teacher's Assignment

- Check Paper Content
Q: Does Evidence Support the Thesis Statement?

- Check Paper Structure
Grammar, Spelling, Punctuation, and Neatness

- Hire a Professional Editor to Find Fatal Flaws

- Daily Back Ups on External Hard Drives

Steps to Success

Step 1. Read Assignment Again to Check Requirements
Read assignment sheet again to be sure that you understand fully what is expected of you, and that your essay/research paper meets requirements as specified by your teacher.

Step 2. Let Paper Rest and Read It with Fresh Eyes
If you let the paper sit for a few days, you will later be able to read it from a new perspective and find the remaining flaws, either in structure or content.

Step 3. Use SMARTGRADES Proofreading Tools (Chapter 8) Use proofreading checklist to correct structural or contextual errors in your paper.

Step 4. Ask a Third Party Editor to Read Your Paper
Find an online editor to read your paper and offer valuable corrections and suggestions. E-mail your paper to the professional editor, and specify a deadline that is at least two weeks before the due-date of your paper. This way, if there is a setback, you will still have time to find another editor in the nick of time to read and correct any fatal flaws.

Step 5. Print Two Copies of Your Paper
Before you hand in your paper to a teacher, make sure that you have a hard copy of your paper in case the teacher misplaces it or loses it (it happens). When your paper is returned to you, throw away your copy.

Step 6. Make Daily Back-Ups on an External Hard Drive
Make sure that you make daily back ups on an external hard drive of the work that is on your computer. There are countless horror stories of students whose computers crashed, and of research papers that were destroyed.

The Final Draft of Paper
Time Log
Estimate Time: 10 Hours
Actual Time:
Error:
Speedbumps: Any Delays, Detours, and Distractions?

Checklist to Write an A Grade Paper ☑

☑ **Step 1. The Essay Question**

Q: Did you answer the question asked by restating the essay question as the introductory sentence of your essay?

☑ **Step 2. Thesis Statement**

Q: Did you write a Thesis statement (defend a position)?

☑ **Step 3. Research Topic**

Q: Did you choose a researchable topic?

1. Use encyclopedia for a general overview of topic
2. Find experts in field
3. Read primary source materials (autobiographical)
4. Read secondary source materials (biographical)
5. List pro and con arguments
6. Add direct and indirect quotes from experts

☑ **Step 4. Use Critical Thinking Tools (Chapter 7)**

Q: Did you use your **SMARTGRADES** Critical Thinking Tools to separate facts from opinion of the author?

☑ **Step 5. Write Outline**

Q: Did you write an Outline of the main ideas and supporting examples to properly organize your research?

☑ **Step 6. Use Standard Paper Structure**

Q: Did you use standard paper structure: Introduction, Body, and Conclusion?

☑ **Step 7. Use Standard Paragraph Structure**

Q: Did you use standard paragraph structure: Introductory sentence, quote from expert, supporting examples, analysis, and concluding sentence?

☑ **Step 8. Paraphrase Don't Plagiarize**

Q: Did you paraphrase (write out ideas in your own words)?

☑ **Step 9. Use Transition Words**

Q: Did you use transition words to bridge paragraphs and link ideas within paragraphs? e.g., According to, For example, In addition, As a result, and In conclusion.

☑ **Step 10. Add Citations and Bibliography**

Q: Did you use citations to document your sources?

☑ **Step 11. Proofread Paper to Perfection**

Q: Did you use your **SMARTGRADES** Proofreading Tools?

As Long as the World is
Turning and Spinning,
We're Gonna Be Dizzy and
We're Gonna Make Mistakes

Mel Brooks

Proofread Paper to Perfection

Proofread Papers to Perfection

Tools of the Trade

Proofreading to Perfection
- ☐ Time and Patience
- ☐ Enlarging Text
- ☐ Reading Aloud
- ☐ Computer Proofreading Software, e.g., Acrobat

Proofread for Content
- ☐ Check Outline
- ☐ Check Research Material
- ☐ Check Paper Format
- ☐ Check Thesis Statement
- ☐ Check Organization of Ideas
- ☐ Check Redundancy
- ☐ Check Writing Style
- ☐ Check Facts
- ☐ Check Paraphrasing
- ☐ Check Fallacies
- ☐ Check Quotes
- ☐ Check Citation Format

Proofread for Writing Mechanics
- ☐ Check Spelling
- ☐ Check Grammar
- ☐ Check Punctuation
- ☐ Check Paragraph Format
- ☐ Check Sentences
- ☐ Check Word Usage
- ☐ Check Wordiness
- ☐ Check Clichés
- ☐ Check Word Repetition
- ☐ Check Gender
- ☐ Check 3 Nevers
- ☐ Check Neatness

Steps to Success

Step 1. Proofreading Takes Time
Proofreading is a time-intensive task. Set aside at least five to ten hours to read through your paper to proofread it to perfection.

Step 2. Enlarge Text
Your writing software allows you to enlarge the font from 12 to 22 points. You will then be able to see the smallest error, e.g., a comma that is supposed to be a period.

Step 3. Read Aloud
It is easier to find typos when you read your paper aloud. Your ears can find errors that your eyes cannot see.

Step 4. Read Aloud Computer Software
Some computers have speech software programs such as Text Edit or Adobe Acrobat software. These programs will read the paper back to you and locate writing errors.

Proofread for Writing Mechanics

Proofread for Spelling
Q: Did you use computer spellchecker to find spelling errors?

Proofread for Grammar
Q: Did you read for past, present, and future tenses?
Q: Did you keep the tenses in the present tense?

Proofread for Punctuation
Q: Did you check for capitalization of proper nouns, comma overuse, and for periods that stay inside the quotes?

Proofread for Paragraph Format
Q: Did you check for transition words, topic sentence, one main idea per paragraph, supporting examples, quote from expert in the field, analysis that uses your critical thinking skills, and concluding sentence?

Proofread for Sentences
Q: Did you check for sentence fragments, run-ons, or comma splices (change punctuation or add a conjunction).

Proofread for Word Usage
Q: Did you use the thesaurus to find the best word to communicate your ideas and express your exact meaning?

Q: Did you eliminate wordiness?

Q: Did you avoid clichés?

Proofread for Repetition
Q: Did you use the same word over and over again?

Proofread for Gender
Q: Is your use of masculine and feminine pronouns like "he" or "she" appropriate?

Proofread for 3 Nevers
Never begin a sentence with "and" or "because."
Never include personal opinions.
Never use "I" in essays.

Proofread for Neatness
Q: Did you use the correct margins, double spacing, font, and paper?

Proofread for Outline
Q: Does your paper correspond to your original outline?

Proofread for Research
Q: Are your primary and secondary sources credible?

Proofread for Paper Format
Q: Does your paper have an Introduction, Body, and Conclusion?

Proofread for Thesis Statement
Q: Is your Thesis clearly stated in your introduction?

Proofread for Organization of Ideas
First give major points, and then give minor points.

Proofread for Redundancy
Q: Did you make the same point more than once?

Proofread for Writing Style
Q: Is your writing style appropriate for the required assignment, e.g., creative, scholarly or scientific?

Proofread for Facts
Q: Does your evidence really back up your argument?
Is all the information relevant to your thesis statement?

Proofread for Paraphrasing
Q: Did you rewrite facts in your own words, and document sources?

Proofread for Fallacies (defects that weaken arguments):
Sweeping generalizations, appeal to authority, weak analogy, or ad populum.

Proofread for Quotes
Q: Are your quotes properly documented in an endnote, or in a footnote and in a bibliography?

Proofread for Citation Format
Q: Are your citations correctly formatted: APA, MLA, or Chicago

Let's Recap: SMARTGRADES Proofreading Checklist

Q: Did you set aside large blocks of time to proofread your paper to perfection?

Q: Did you enlarge the text to font size 18 to magnify your errors and make them easily visible?

Q: Did you choose font size 18 to find typos?

Q: Did you read your paper out loud to readily weed out all the errors?

Q: Did you purchase speech recognition software to cut in half the time it takes to proofread?

Q: Does paper correspond to your original outline?

Q: Does paper have an Introduction, Body, and Conclusion?

Q: Is your Thesis Statement clearly stated in your introduction?

Q: Is your writing style appropriate for the required assignment, e.g., creative, scholarly, or scientific?

Q: Does your evidence really back up your arguments?

Q: Is all the research relevant to your thesis statement?

Check Paraphrasing
Q: Did you rewrite the facts in your own words, and document the sources?

Check Fallacies (defects that weaken arguments)
(a) Sweeping generalizations
(b) Appeal to authority
(c) Weak analogy
(d) Ad populum

Check Quotes
Q: Are your quotes properly documented in an endnote or in a footnote and in a bibliography?

Check Paragraph Format
Q: Did you check for transition words, topic sentence, one main idea per paragraph, supporting example, quote from expert in the field, analysis and critical thinking skills, and concluding sentence?

Check Sentences
Q: Did you check for sentence fragments, run-ons, or comma splices (change punctuation or add conjunction).

Check Word Usage
Q: Did you use the thesaurus to find the best word to communicate your ideas and express your exact meaning?

Check Neatness
Q: Did you use the correct margins, double spacing, font, and paper?

What Is the Hardest Task in the World?
To Think.

Ralph Waldo Emerson

'Thinking," said the little boy,
"is when your mouth stays shut and
your head keeps talking to itself."

Chapter 7
Your Thinking Tools

Critical Thinking Tools
Creative Thinking Tools
Scientific Thinking Tools
Mathematical Thinking Tools

There Is Only One Truth:
NO ONE HAS THE TRUTH

Sharon Esther Lampert
Philosopher, Poet, and Peacemaker

Critical Thinking Tools

The Trouble with the World Is that the Stupid Are Cocksure and the Intelligent Are Full of Doubt

Bertrand Russell

Critical Thinking Tools

Tools of the Trade

1. Read with an Open Mind
2. Read with a Critical Mind
3. Evaluate the Underlying Assumptions
4. Read for Arguments Based on Fallacies
5. Read for Inductive and Deductive Reasoning

Steps to Success

Step 1. Read with an Open Mind
Develop mental flexibility, a willingness to think clearly and weigh all sides of every question. To resolve a problem, attack a problem with an open mind. Prepare to consider all possibilities and probe the issue to the heart.

Step 2. Read with a Critical Mind
Separate the facts of the story (verifiable evidence) from the opinions of the author. Caution: Some facts, such as statistical surveys and historical events are based on "opinions."

Step 3. Evaluate the Underlying Assumptions
Assumptions are the set of belief systems that are considered to be self-evident.

Step 4. Read for Arguments Based on Fallacies
Learn to recognize the presentation of misleading evidence that is false.

Misdirected Appeals: Appeal to authority, appeal to common or popular belief, appeal to common practice or tradition, appeal to indirect consequences, appeal to wishful thinking.

Emotional Appeals: Appeal to fear or scare tactics, appeal to force, appeal to loyalty or peer pressure, appeal to pity or sob story, appeal to prejudice, appeal to stereotypes, appeal to hatred, appeal to vanity.

Step 5. Read for Inductive and Deductive Reasoning
Induction argues from observation from the specific to the general. Deduction argues from the general to the specific (rules and laws).

A Checklist for Critical Thinking Tools

Q: Did you read with an open mind?

Q: Did you think clearly and weigh all sides of every question?

Q: Did you resolve a problem, and attack a problem with a flexible mind?

Q: Did you consider all possibilities and probe the issue to the heart?

Q: Did you read with a critical mind and separate the facts of the story (verifiable evidence) from the opinions of the author.

Q: Did you evaluate the underlying assumptions?

Q: Did you read for arguments based on fallacies?

Misdirected Appeals:
1. Appeal to authority
2. Appeal to common or popular belief
3. Appeal to common practice or tradition
4. Appeal to indirect consequences
5. Appeal to wishful thinking

Emotional Appeals:
1. Appeal to fear or scare tactics
2. Appeal to force
3. Appeal to loyalty or peer pressure
4. Appeal to pity or sob story
5. Appeal to prejudice
6. Appeal to stereotypes
7. Appeal to hatred
8. Appeal to vanity

Q: Did you read for inductive and deductive reasoning?

If I Create from the Heart,
Nearly Everything Works;
If from the Head Almost Nothing

Marc Chagall

Critical Thinking
analytic
convergent
vertical
probability
judgment
focused
objective
answer
left brain
verbal
linear
reasoning
yes but

Creative Thinking
generative
divergent
lateral
possibility
suspended judgment
diffuse
subjective
an answer
right brain
visual
associative
richness, novelty
yes and

Creative Thinking Tools

SEE THE WORLD THROUGH THE EYES OF A CREATIVE GENIUS

POE**T**REE

Ink needs a pen.
Pen needs paper.
Paper needs a poem
Poem needs a poet.
Poet needs a muse.
Muse needs a poet.
Poet needs divine inspiration.
Divine inspiration needs divine intervention.
Divine intervention needs divine grace.
Divine grace needs immortality.
Immortality needs eternity.
Eternity needs readers of poetry.

Sharon Esther Lampert

www.WorldFamousPoems.com
The Greatest Poems Ever Written on Extraordinary World Events

Creative Thinking Tools

10 Tools of the Trade

V.E.S.S.E.L.

INSPIRATION

IMPREGNATION

INCUBATION

GENESIS

SILENT: LISTEN

METAMORPHOSIS

REVELATION

SIGNATURE

IMMORTALITY

Steps to Success

Step 1. V.E.S.S.E.L.
Artistic gifts are inherited, e.g., writers, painters, dancers, and singers. There are good, great, and gifted **ARTISTS**.

Step 2. INSPIRATION
When something moves you emotionally and transforms your inner world in such a way that you feel differently, think differently, and see differently, that external force is called inspiration, e.g., Music, Artwork, Education.

Step 3. IMPREGNATION (ART & ARTWORK BECOME ONE)
Once you have been inspired by something or someone, you have become impregnated with an idea that will eventually manifest into **ART**. The **ART** and the **ARTIST** become one (intangible and invisible) entity.

Step 4. INCUBATION
The **ART** resides within you and grows quietly over time. There is no such thing as "Writer's Block." It is a myth. You must be patient and allow **ART** to incubate within you.

Step 5. GENESIS (ART & ARTWORK SEPARATE INTO TWO)
When **ART** is ready to be born, it takes on a life of its own, separates from the **ARTIST**, and has its own life form and destiny, e.g., a painting, poem, or music composition.

Step 6. SILENT: LISTEN
The **ARTIST** silently listens to the seedling of an **ARTWORK**.

Step 7. METAMORPHOSIS
The **ART** has to be nurtured to reach complete maturity. The **ART** and the **ARTIST** are now separate entities. The **ART** and the **ARTIST** have to be nurtured for both of them to grow, nurture each other, and reach maturity.

Step 8. REVELATION
The **ART** touches other people with its own message and has its distinct own destiny, separate from the artist.

Step 9. SIGNATURE
The **ARTWORK** bears the signature of the **ARTIST**.

Step 10. IMMORTALITY
Great **ART** lives forever beyond the life of the **ARTIST**.
ARTIST IS MORTAL; ART IS IMMORTAL.

Steps to Success

Most creative people credit their vivid imaginations for their success, e.g., J.K. Rowling and Harry Potter.

Q: Do you have the emotional, spiritual, and intellectual fortitude to express your ideas without fear from shame and ridicule?

Q: Do you have a vivid imagination?

Q: Do you write down your wild'n'crazy ideas and let them mature into a poem, a play, or a novel?

Q: Are you a daydreamer? Do you write down your daydreams?

Q: Do you let your mind flow freely to associate and brainstorm for ideas?

DAILY ACTION PLAN

Creative thinking requires thinking "outside the box." Start a creative ideas journal. List all ideas that come to mind, no matter how bizarre, weird, or strange, and see where they take you. Perhaps a novel will emerge, or a poem, or a plot for a movie script or even a play.

Theory Guides. Experiment Decides.

Scientific Thinking Tools

Scientific Thinking Tools

The scientific method is a process for experimentation that is used to explore observations that use the five senses, and to answer questions about the natural world. Scientists use the scientific method to search for cause and effect relationships in nature. An experiment is designed so that changes to one item cause something else to vary in a predictable way. The sciences rely heavily on numbers as data, and on replicable experimentation to measure and calculate results.

Tools of the Trade

The Scientific Method
- Make Observations By Using Your 5 Senses
- Ask Questions
- Perform Experiments
- Collect Data
- Measure Data
- Classify Data
- Make a Hypothesis
- Interpret Data
- Analyze Information
- Draw Conclusions
- Make a Prediction
- Verification of Experiment

The Science Report

Section 1.   Title Page
Section 2.   Abstract
Section 3.   Table of Contents
Section 4.   Question, Variables, and Hypothesis
Section 5.   Background Research
Section 6.   Materials List
Section 7.   Experimental Procedure
Section 8.   Data Analysis and Discussion
Section 9.   Conclusions
Section 10. Ideas for Future Research
Section 11. Acknowledgements
Section 12. Bibliography

Q: What Is Scientific Thinking?
Scientific (and critical) thinking is based on three things:
1. **Empiricism:** Using empirical evidence found in nature. Using evidence that is found in nature. It is evidence that is perceptible from the senses; evidence that one can see, hear, touch, taste, or smell.

2. **Rationalism:** Practicing logical reasoning

3. **Skepticism:** Possessing a skeptical attitude about presumed knowledge that leads to self-questioning, holding tentative conclusions, and being undogmatic (willingness to change one's beliefs).

WORLD PEACE EQUATION

VG+VL=VP

Virtue of the Good + Value of Life = Vision of Peace

The Mathematical and Philosophical Proof for World Peace

$$VG + VL = VP$$
$$VP = VG + VL$$
$$VP = V(G+L)$$
$$P = (G+L)$$
$$\text{Peace} = \text{Good} + \text{Life}$$
$$\text{Peace} = \text{Goodlife}$$

PHOTON
SUPERHERO OF EDUCATION
www.BooksNotBombs.com

SMART POWER IS BACK IN THE HANDS OF ALL STUDENTS

Mathematical Thinking Tools

The Highest Form of Pure Thought Is in Mathematics

Plato
Ancient Greek Philosopher
428 BC-348 BC

Mathematical Thinking Tools

Math is learned by solving many types of problems. Math is cumulative. Every class builds on the previous one.

Tools of the Trade

Solving Math Problems
1. Think in steps: Step by step
2. Memorize the fundamentals
3. Translate abstract concepts into concrete terms

Ask Questions
1. What is given?
2. What is called for?
3. How many steps are required?
4. What operation must be used in each step?
5. Are the steps in the right order?
6. Check answer and make sure it is right

Math Errors
20% of All Math Errors Are Careless Mistakes
1. Write each number legibly
2. Place two columns of figures exactly under one another
3. Copy each problem correctly

Steps to Success

In-Class Math Strategy: Take Organized Math Notes
Keep a list of the types of math problems solved and the sequence of steps:

Math Problem Type   Equations Used   Sequence of Steps

- As questions arise, ask your teacher for clarification.
- Don't leave class feeling lost, confused, and hopeless.

At-Home Math Strategy: Rework Class Problems
After every class, review your class notes and rework the math problems covered in class

Step 1. Write Out the Math Problem
- Read the word problem slowly and carefully.

- Remember this adage: Go slow to go fast.

- Slow is the way to accuracy and great grades.

- Write out the problem, number the steps, and double check what you've written.

- What are you trying to figure out? The last sentence of a word problem tells you what you are trying to find.

Step 2. Write Down the Information in the Problem

Data   Variable   Equation

Word problems contain all the information needed to answer the question.

- List all the information given in the problem.

- Make two lists: Separate the knowns from the unknowns (the variable).

        Knowns   **Unknowns**

Q: What is the relationship between the known and the unknown values?

- Write an equation.

- Solve for the unknowns.

Step 3. What is the Best Math Method?
Make a plan and solve the problem. Develop a plan to solve the problem and solve it according to your plan.

Q: How many steps does it take to solve the problem?

Q: Does one part of the problem have to be solved before other parts can be solved?

Q: Can the problem be divided into parts and solved separately?

Step 4. Check Your Work and Reread the Problem

- Check to see that you did not leave out any steps of your plan.

- Read problem again to see if your answer makes sense.

- Check answers for careless mistakes.

- Double check your calculator work immediately.

Step 5. Math Test Success Strategy

- Solve unassigned homework problems and see if you can finish them in the allotted time for the exam.

- Write big and bold. This will allow you to see a mistake and keep from confusing numbers, letters, or signs. Careless errors often creep in because you don't give your self enough space to see and solve the problem.

- Answer the easy questions first to build your confidence. Budget your time.

- If you get stuck on a problem move on and come back to it later.

- Don't leave if you finish the exam early. Go back to the difficult problems.

- Use all of the available time to look for careless errors.

If You Think Dogs Can't Count,
Try Putting Three Dog Biscuits in Your Pocket
and Then Giving Fido Only Two of Them.

Phil Pastoret

Little Johnny

Little Johnny was sitting in class doing math problems when his teacher picked him to answer a question, "Johnny, if there were five birds sitting on a fence and you shot one with your gun, how many would be left?" "None," replied Johnny, "cause the rest would fly away." "Well, the answer is four," said the teacher, "but I like the way you're thinking."

**Be Nice to Nerds!
Chances Are, You'll End Up Working for One!**
Bill Gates
CEO of Microsoft

Chapter 8
What Do You Want to Be When You Grow Up

Follow Your Passion,
Fulfill Your Potential, and
Find Your Place in the World

PHOTON
SUPERHERO OF EDUCATION
EVERYBODY IS SOMEBODY SPECIAL
www.PhotonSuperhero.com

What Do You Want to Be When You Grow Up

Everybody is somebody special. Before you can find out how special you are, you have to figure out your strengths and weaknesses.

My Strengths Are:
1. _____
2. _____
3. _____

My Weaknesses Are:
1. _____
2. _____
3. _____

Once you have a clear picture of yourself, you will then be able to make choices that lead you in the direction of your dreams. For example, if you love science because you want to know how the natural world works, then you will probably read a lot of books about biology, chemistry, and physics. The key to success is to align your personality with a career that will become your life's work and passion. Everyone in the world does the same thing, that is, everyone is a "caretaker" of something in the world. Some people become florists because they like to care for flowers. Some people become mechanics because they love to care for cars. To find your passion, ask yourself this simple question: Q: What do want to take care of?

My Passion Is: _____.

How to Choose a Career That Fits Your Personality Type

Read through the lists below for careers that are interesting to you and that will need futher exploration to acertain whether you are well suited based on your intellectual and emotional strengths and weaknesses.

Hands-On Career Choices (for the physically active)
Air Traffic Controller, Archaeologist, Athletic Trainer, Carpenter, Caterer, Cartographer, Chef, Computer Repairs Engineer Construction Worker, Dental Technician, Drafter, Electrician, Farm Manager, Firefighter, Fish and Game Warden, Forester, Hairdresser, Landscape Architect, Licensed Practical Nurse, Locksmith, Mechanic, Machinist, Military Officer, Physical Therapist, Police Officer, Plumber, Recreation Administrator, Surveyor, Teacher, Truck Driver, X-Ray Technician

Helper Career Choices
(working with people, good communicators)
Airline Personnel, Athletic Coach, Attorney, Career Counselor, Chamber of Commerce Claims Adjuster, Child Care Worker, Cosmetologist, Counselor, Dietitian, Fitness Instructor, Funeral Director, Home Health Aide, Information Clerk, Occupational Therapist, Mental Health Specialist, Nurse, Office Worker Paramedic, Parole Officer, Personnel Director, Physical Therapist, Receptionist, Recreation Director, Religious Worker, Teacher, Therapist, Travel Agent, Sales Representative, Social Worker, Waiter/Waitress, Youth Service Worker

Investigator Career Choices
(curious, logical, think independently, work alone)
Astronomer, Biologist, College Professor, Computer Analyst, Computer System Analyst, Consumer Researcher, Dentist, Dietitian, Ecologist, Engineer, Horticulturist, Lawyer, Librarian, Medical Technologist, Meteorologist, Nurse, Paralegal, Pharmacist, Physician, Police Detective, Reporter, Research Analyst, Science Lab Technician, Science/Math Teacher, Technical Writer, Veterinarian

Helper Career Choices
(working with people, good communicators)
Airline Personnel, Athletic Coach, Attorney Career Counselor, Chamber of Commerce Claims Adjuster, Child Care Worker, Cosmetologist, Counselor, Dietitian, Fitness Instructor, Funeral Director, Home Health Aide Information Clerk, Occupational Therapist Mental Health Specialist, Nurse, Office Worker Paramedic, Parole Officer, Personnel Director Physical Therapist, Receptionist, Recreation Director, Religious Worker, Teacher, Therapist, Travel Agent, Sales Representative, Social Worker, Waiter/Waitress, Youth Service Worker

Enterprise Career Choices
(outgoing, self-confident, sociable, adventurous)
Advertising Agent, Advertising Executive, Announcer, Banker, Business Manager, Campaign Manager, Entrepreneur, Florist, Insurance Manager, Lawyer, Lobbyist, Office Manager, Personnel Recruiter, Police Officer, Politician, Real Estate Appraiser, Sales Person, Stock Broker, Travel Agent, TV/Radio

Artist Career Choices
(self-expression, imaginative, innovative)

Advertising Manager, Architect, Artist, Cartographer, Cosmetologist, Dance Instructor, Drama Coach, English Teacher, Entertainer, Florist, Graphic Designer, Interior Decorator, Illustrator, Journalist, Landscaper, Librarian, Lighting Specialist, Museum Curator, Music Teacher, Musician, Painter, Photographer Recording Technician, Reporter, Writer

Science Career Choices
(curious, logical, think independently, work alone)

Aerospace Engineer, Astronomer, Aviation Inspector, Athletic Trainer, Biochemist, CAD Technician, Chemist, Civil Engineer, Computer Hardware Engineer, Computer Programmer, Computer Software Engineer, Diver, Electrical Engineer Electrician, Environmental Engineer, Food Science Technician Food Scientist or Technologist, Genetic Counselor, Geographer, Geologist, Industrial Engineer, Marine Architect, Mechanical Engineer, Medical and Clinical Laboratory Technician, Meteorologist, Microbiologist, Multi-Media Artist or Animator, Natural Sciences Manager, Physicist, Pilot, Plant Scientist, Psychologist, Ship and Boat Captain, Sociologist, Sound Engineering Technician, Statistician, Veterinarian, Zoologist, Wildlife Biologist.

Detailers Career Choices
(steady routines, defined procedures, collecting and organizing)

Accountant, Actuary, Administrative Assistant, Auditor Statistician, Bank Manager, Business Teacher, Librarian, Bookkeeper, Cartographer, Cashier, Credit Manager, CAD Operator, Coat Analyst, Corrections Officer, Computer Operator, Court Reporter, Estimator, Financial Analyst, Hotel Clerk, Insurance Underwriter, Medical Lab Technologist, Medical Secretary, Personnel Clerk, Secretary, Paralegal, Proofreader, Reservations Agent, Safety Inspector, Tax Consultant

Know Thyself

1. What type of career is best suited to your personality type?

2. What social causes are you most concerned about?

3. If you could change something in the world, what would it be?

4. Where do you think you can make a difference?

5. When kinds of books do you love to read?

"What If you could solve just one problem in this world and by solving that one problem you could solve every problem in the world?

If we just solve the "problem of education," then we could solve every problem in the world: poverty, illiteracy, domestic violence, religious strife, and war.

The human brain is the most powerful biological machine in the world. What would the world look like if educators knew how to nurture and cultivate the awesome power of the human brain?

When the seeds of peace are planted within the minds and hearts of our children, through education, then and only then, will there be peace on earth. Our children are our only hope for peace in the world, and education is the only path to peace."

Sharon Rose Sugar
The Paladin of Education for the 21st Century

THIS BOOK SAVES LIVES
"The Silent Crisis Destroying America's Brightest Minds"
"Book of the Month" Alma Public Library, Wisconsin

About Us

SMARTGRADES
BRAIN POWER REVOLUTION

Sharon Rose Sugar
The Paladin of Education for the 21st Century

Critical Contributions to Education

1. **SMARTGRADES: BRAIN POWER REVOLUTION**
2. Education Paradigm: The Learning-Processing Education System
3. 40 Universal Gold Standards of Education
4. How to Nurture and Cultivate the Power of the Human Brain?
5. How Does Learning Take Place?
6. How to Measure Education?

7. 8 Goalposts of Education:
    1. EDUCATION: KNOWLEDGE!
    2. ENLIGHTENMENT: AHA!
    3. EMPOWERMENT: YES I CAN!
    4. EXCELLENCE: MASTERY!
    5. EMANCIPATION: ALL CAN DO!
    6. EGALITARIANISM: EQUAL RIGHTS!
    7. EQUALITY: NEW WORLD ORDER!
    8. ECONOMIC STABILITY: WORLD PEACE!

8. Integration Therapy for Intrapersonal Growth, Development, and Maturity: The 13 Steps to True and Everlasting Happiness

9. Feed the Whole Child: Mind, Body, and Spirit
10. Spiritual Affirmations: Empowerment, Responsibility, Special Gifts

11. The Silent Crisis Destroying America's Brightest Minds
    - The 15 Stumbling Blocks of Academic Failure
    - The 15 Stepping Stones to Academic Success
    - The Downward Spiral of Academic Failure
    - Academic Insanity
    - The Misdiagnosis of A.D.H.D., "The Incurable Brain Disorder"

12. The 3 Stages of Child Abuse: Cripple, Parasite, and Predator

13. Coined Word, "Democrisy," a Democracy Laden with Hypocrisy

14. PHOTON: Superhero of Education, PhotonSuperhero.com

15. C.A.P.S. Children's Science Curriculum, Grades 1-4

16. In One Hour, Read Hebrew, HebrewPowerHour.com

Thinkers in Education

One Small Step for Women and One Giant Leap Forward for Education and World Peace.

Alain, Aristotle, Avicenna, Bello, Bettelheim, Binet, Blonsky, Al-Boustani, Buber, Cai Yuanpei, Claparede, Comenious, Condorcet, Confucius, Cousinet, Dawid, Decroly, Dewey, Diesterweg, Durkheim, Eotvos, Erasmus, Al-Farabi, Ferriere, Freinet, Freire, Freud, Frobel, Fukuzawa, Gandhi, Al-Ghazali, Giner de los Rios, Glinos, Goodman, Gramsci, Grundtvig, Grzegorzewska, Hegel, Herbart, Humbolt, Husen, Hussein, Illich, Jaspers, Jovellanos, Jullien de Paris, Kandel, Kant, Kerschensteiner, Key, Ibn Khaldun, Kold, Korczak, Krupskaya, Locke, Makarenko, Marti, Mencious, Miskawayh, Montaigne, Montessori, More, Naik, Neill, Noikov, Nyerere, Ortega y Gasset, Owen, Pestalozzi, Piaget, Plato, Priestley, Al-Qabbani, Read, Rogers, Rousseau, Rudenschold, Sadler, Salomon, Sarmiento, Sergio, Skinner, Spencer, Steiner, Suchodolski, **Sharon Rose Sugar (Sharon Esther Lampert)**, Sun Yat-Sen, Tagore, Al-Tahtawi, Tolstoy, Trefort, Trstenjak, Ushinsky, Uznadze, Varela, Vasconcelos, Vico, Vives, Vygotsky, Wallon

The Official Emblem of

PHOTON
SUPERHERO OF EDUCATION

Super Hero Refresher Course

Clark Kent Is Superman

Bruce Wayne Is Batman

Peter Parker Is Spiderman

Diana Themyscira Is Wonder Woman

Sharon Rose Sugar Is Photon

SMART POWER IS BACK IN THE HANDS OF ALL STUDENTS

PHOTON'S
Spiritual Illuminations

5 SUPER POWERS
MAKE YOUR DREAMS COME TRUE

1. TIME Is Nonrefundable
(Don't Waste Your Time)

2. ENERGY Is Rechargeable
(Stick to a Regular Bedtime)

3. MONEY Travels in a Circle
(You Have to Be in the Loop)

4. SELF-WORTH Is Infinite Potential
(Know Your Strengths, Iron Out Your Weaknesses)

5. LOVE Everything You Touch
(Put Your Heart into Everything)

EVERYBODY IS SOMEBODY SPECIAL
www.BooksNotBombs.com

SMART POWER IS BACK IN THE HANDS OF ALL STUDENTS

PHOTON'S
Spiritual Illuminations

My Empowerment Affirmation

I have only one life.
My life is a valuable gift.
I am responsible for my destiny.
I changed my life to ensure my happiness.
Each day is lived fully with
purpose, enthusiasm, and joy.

EVERYBODY IS SOMEBODY SPECIAL
www.BooksNotBombs.com

SMART POWER IS BACK IN THE HANDS OF ALL STUDENTS

Photon's Spiritual Illuminations

My Circle of Responsibility Affirmation

My Problems Have Solutions
When I Take
RESPONSIBILITY
for my problems have solutions
when I take responsibility for
my problems have solutions
when I take responsibility for
my problems have solutions
when I take responsibility for
my problems have solutions
when I take responsibility for
my problems have solutions
when I take responsibility for
my problems have solutions
when I take responsibility for
my problems have solutions
when I take responsibility for
my problems have solutions
when I take responsibility for
my problems have solutions
When I Take
RESPONSIBILITY.

EVERYBODY IS SOMEBODY SPECIAL
www.BooksNotBombs.com

SMART POWER IS BACK IN THE HANDS OF ALL STUDENTS

Photon's Spiritual Illuminations

My Special Gifts

Inside of Me Are

SPECIAL GIFTS

I am able to use my special gifts,
If I focus on my positive qualities.

I am ready to use my special gifts,
to enhance the quality of my life.

I will use my special gifts for myself,
my loved ones, and to benefit humanity.

EVERYBODY IS SOMEBODY SPECIAL
www.BooksNotBombs.com

SEE THE WORLD THROUGH THE EYES OF A CREATIVE GENIUS

POETRY WORLD RECORD
120 WORDS OF RHYME FROM ONE FAMILY OF RHYME
Bible: "Through the Eyes of Eve"

THE WORLD TRADE CENTER TRAGEDY
"Spiraling Downward, Upward We Stand United"

Dr. Martin Luther King Jr.
"THE DELIVERER"

SIMON WIESENTHAL: NAZI HUNTER
"A Survivor's Burden"

Bible: CAIN & ABEL
"Cain & Abel: Inseparable-Together Forever"

"TSUNAMI" (Poet's Personal Favorite)

SUICIDE BOMBERS
"The Militant Palestinian Toddler Terrorist"

DARFUR
"There Is No Flower in Darfur"

THE IRAQ WAR
"Sandstorm in Baghdad"

KANSAS TWISTER
"The Return of Dorothy Gale"

KATRINA
"Drowning in the American Dream"

CENTRAL PARK VIOLENCE AGAINST WOMEN
"Water, Fight, Flight, and Tears"
(most published poem on the internet)

THE NEW YORK CITY BLACKOUT
"The Return of the Cavewoman"

Does Your Kid Read Sharon Esther Lampert?

Critical Contributions to Civilization

The Prodigy
Unleash The Creator The God Within
10 Esoteric Laws of Genius & Creativity

The Awesome Art of Alliteration
Using One Letter of the Alphabet

The Prophet
Who Knew God Was Such a Chatterbox

THE 22 COMMANDMENTS
All You Will Ever Need to Know About God

The Philosopher Queen
- God of What? 11 Esoteric Laws of Inextricability
- The Sperm Manifesto: 10 Rules for the Road
- Women Have All The Power —
  But Have Never Learned How to Use It

The Poet
- I Stole All The Words from The Dictionary

- **IMMORTALITY IS MINE**
  The Greatest Poems Ever Written on Extraordinary World Events

- **POETRY JEWELS**
  Diamonds, Emeralds, Sapphires, Rubies, and Pearls

- **V.E.S.S.E.L.**
  Very. Extra. Special. Sharon. Esther. Lampert.

How to Read a Poem By Sharon Esther Lampert

1. Similar to the poet William Blake, Sharon's poems are accompanied by elaborate visual graphics that enrich and compliment the text.

2. Sharon is a master of the art of condensation. She is able to condense a major world event in world history into a one page poem.

3. Sharon's poems are telescopic of the main event and microscopic of the infinite details.

4. Sharon's poems are known for her ability to weave poetry, philosophy, and comedy into a single verse.

5. Sharon's poems take you on a cinematic journey, and make you feel as if you are reliving the event, as if it happened today.

6. Many poets leave abandoned poems, that are unfinished. Sharon's poems are completed works of art. Every word is essential to the poem. You cannot remove or replace a word. There are no extra words. Every word has its rightful place and fits to perfection.

7. Sharon's poems are inspired. There are no rough drafts. Like giving birth to a baby, the poem incubates in her "creative apparatus" and is birthed in minutes. Like a baby, the poems are delivered whole and complete.

8. The last verse of every poem delivers a message that educates, enlightens, and empowers. Her searing signature endings seep under your skin, and find a way into your heart, and open your mind to a deeper understanding of the world.

Letter from Mommy, Age 9
Darling Sharon,
My Daughter is a Poet, Philosopher,
and Teacher.
Beauty & Brains.
Love and Kisses, XXX
Mommy (Eve Lampert)

Remarks from Abraham Lampert: "My Daughter Is "FABRENT" (Yiddish: born with a fire burning under the tushee)

SHARON ESTHER LAMPERT

The Sole Intention of My Poetry Is to Add Light to Your Soul.
Sharon Esther Lampert

SEE THE WORLD THROUGH THE EYES OF A CREATIVE GENIUS

APRIL 30
NYC Poetry In Your Pocket Day

BE BORN

Be Born.
Become Educated.
Love Your Work.
Make a Meaningful Contribution -
To Yourself, Your Family, and Humanity.
Be a True Friend to Yourself First.
Have Sex with Someone You Love.
Make Love with Complete Abandon.
Enjoy Unconditional Love from Your Devoted Pet.
Make Time to Read the Funnies and Laugh.
Save Enough Money to Visit the Popular,
Pretty, and Peaceful Places of the World.
Read Great Literature, Listen to Great Music,
See Great Art, Watch the Great Movies,
Play the Fun Sports, Dance till Dawn,
Taste the Great Culinary Delights of the World -
Eat Slowly, Enjoy Every Bite, and Stay in Shape.
Plan One Great Adventure and Stick to the Plan.
Grow Old and Wise. Leave Your Money to
Someone You Love - Who Loves You Back.
Die in Your Sleep.

Sharon Esther Lampert

www.WorldFamousPoems.com
The Greatest Poems Ever Written on Extraordinary World Events

The Sole Intention of My Poetry Is to Add **LIGHT** to Your Soul

SEE THE WORLD THROUGH THE EYES OF A CREATIVE GENIUS

THE 22 COMMANDMENTS
ALL YOU WILL EVER NEED TO KNOW ABOUT GOD
A UNIVERSAL MORAL COMPASS FOR ALL PEOPLE,
FOR ALL RELIGIONS, AND FOR ALL TIME

1. LIFE Over Death
2. STRENGTH Over Weakness
3. DEED Over Sin
4. LOVE Over Hatred
5. TRUTH Over Lie
6. WISDOM Over Stupidity
7. OPTIMISM Over Pessimism
8. SHARING Over Selfishness
9. PRAISE Over Criticism
10. LOYALTY Over Abandonment
11. RESPONSIBILITY Over Blame
12. GRATITUDE Over Envy
13. REWARD Over Punishment
14. ALLIES Over Enemies
15. CREATION Over Destruction
16. EDUCATION Over Ignorance
17. COOPERATION Over Competition
18. FREEDOM Over Oppression
19. COMPASSION Over Indifference
20. FORGIVENESS Over Revenge
21. PEACE Over War
22. JOY Over Suffering

Sharon Esther Lampert
Kadimah: 8th Prophetess of Israel

www.PoetryJewels.com
Diamonds, Emeralds, Sapphires, Rubies, and Pearls

The Sole Intention of My Poetry Is to Add **LIGHT** to Your Soul

Our Education Websites

SMARTGRADES
BRAIN POWER REVOLUTION
Smartgrades.com
EveryDayAnEasyA.com

PHOTON
SUPERHERO OF EDUCATION
EVERYBODY IS SOMEBODY SPECIAL
PhotonSuperhero.com

THE SMARTEST CHILDREN'S BOOK IN THE
WHOLE WORLD
(Color-Coded Vocabulary Words)

SCHMALTZY
In America, Even a Cat Can Have a Dream
Schmaltzy.com